The Poets' Theatre Series

THREE

PASSAGES FROM FINNEGANS WAKE

BY JAMES JOYCE

A Free Adaptation for the Theater

by Mary Manning

1957 · *HARVARD UNIVERSITY PRESS*
CAMBRIDGE, MASSACHUSETTS

FINNEGANS WAKE

The first stage presentation of this adaptation was at The Poets' Theatre in Cambridge, Massachusetts, on April 25, 1955.

Typography by Burton L. Stratton. The type used is English Monotype Fournier No. 185. Composition, presswork, and binding by the Plimpton Press, Norwood, Massachusetts, U.S.A.

For

STEPHEN JOYCE

"Loud, heap miseries upon us yet entwine
our arts with laughters low!"

INTRODUCTION

By Denis Johnston

Finnegans Wake is a book that everybody knows about, but that few — apart from professionals — can honestly claim to have read. To do so from beginning to end, allowing no sentence to pass without reasonable consideration, while keeping the tortured mind concentrated upon the matter in hand, is a feat of strength that is generally supposed to require an ideal insomnia. A worse description could hardly be invented, since the book itself has the quality of making sleep impossible, and nothing can more surely guarantee a restless night than half an hour with it as a bedside book. As a waking-up book, on the other hand, I have found it splendid.

Yet the trouble in reading it is oddly out of line with the fact that few works of literature keep trying so continuously to explain themselves to the reader. Page after page of self-criticism and confession is couched in language that demands to be reread three or four times before the multiple sense strikes home, and this is as strange a paradox as the fact that the author, who must have been one of the vainest men on earth, keeps warning us that he is a charlatan — a piece of masochistic self-abuse that is actually the most fraudulent thing about him.

We must also remember that Joyce was a man already half blind when writing the *Wake*, but with a wonderful ear for music. Consequently, large sections are not intended for the eye at all, but for the ear. It has a rhythm, and sometimes even a rhyme that demands to be read aloud.

> His bludgeon's bruk, his drum is tore. For spuds we'll keep the hat he wore And roll in clover on his clay By wather parted from the say.

Many of its tricks with words —

> Wring out the clothes. Wring in the dew. Godavari vert the showers —

are hardly visible upon the page, and only come to light when spoken. This applies in particular to a mass of puns based upon the pronunciation of languages and dialects other than standard English, particularly the Gaelic — "They called her Holly Merry, her lips were so ruddyberry"; and "Roman Pathoricks."

It is not surprising, therefore, that the best approach to an early appreciation of the *Wake* is to see it performed. In deference to its liturgical qualities, it would probably be at its best sung as a Midnight Mass, were it not for the difficulty that it would be noon long before the ceremony was over. So Mary Manning has done the next best thing, by providing us with this dramatization which, when performed, enables us to leap a great many of the preliminary hurdles, and to enjoy its general flavor without the aid of any Keys.

In her very first problem, however — that of cutting the text down to a manageable length — she must inevitably throw enough fat in the fire to scald herself to death. Because, to every independent lover of this "cantrap of fermented words," the book as a whole must mean something different, and usually something that is particularly personal. The tome has both literary and historical aspects. It is an autobiographical document as well as an architectural and geographical Blue Guide to Ireland. It has profound religious significance, never yet fully analyzed, as well as being one of the dirtiest books in print. To some, it is an attack on De Valera, while to others its conclusion amounts to a plea for color television.

So whatever line Miss Manning takes — and she has got to take some line — she will inevitably call down upon her head the criticism that she has distorted the principal theme of the work. But this will only beg the question as to what the principal theme is.

It is very tempting to try to set out in so-called simple language just what Joyce was getting at in the *Wake*, but one has only to look at the various attempts that are already in print to see that, as a rule, they only succeed in making the book seem pretentiously dull. Moreover, it is an act that we have been expressly warned against by the master himself, who describes the process as:

> Unconsciously explaining, for inkstands, with a meticulosity bordering on the insane, the various meanings of all the different foreign parts of speech he misused and cuttlefishing every lie unshrinkable about all the other people in the story, leaving out, of course, foreconsciously the simple worf and

plague and poison . . . until there was not a snoozer among them but was utterly undeceived in the heel of the reel by the recital of the rigmarole.

So Mary Manning — than whom nobody could be less like a cuttlefish — has concentrated on what she regards as the simple worf and plague (and poison, if you insist) of the story, presenting it basically as a resurrection dream, in which the answer to the mystery of death is given by the woman-river, Anna Livia Plurabelle — this image of sentient experience that flows from source to mouth, is lost in the ocean, and yet, miraculously, continues to flow.

The book itself has no reluctance in telling us several times over what, precisely, it professes to be — a new presentation of the Tiberiast Duplex (Joyce's term for the double-talk originating by the Lake of Galilee that has lain so long buried in the sloblands of Clontarf that it is now illegible) — a rewritten Tunc-page for the Book of Kells, that the author considers necessary for every Finnegan who, having fallen off his ladder, hopes to rise again with a whiff of the Holy Spirit.

It will be seen that this is no inconsiderable purpose. Indeed, it is hardly surprising that Joyce, with a very proper embarrassment over his own pretensions, has attempted to conceal his meaning in a good deal of double-talk of his own, so enabling him to leave this mortal sphere, before his full intention was found out. His claim, however, to be admitted to the role of the prophets is, perhaps, supported by the fact that his book manages to draw the material of its dreams — Dunne-like — not only from the past, but from the future, too. It is already a matter of puzzlement to some commentators that, although there are only three chapters that were not already partially in print as long ago as the early thirties, we find, scattered throughout its pages, references to the holocaust of the second war, to collaborators, to Existentialism, to events yet-to-be in his own family, and even to his own death — "evacuated at the mere appearance of three germhuns" to where "he collapsed carefully under a bedtick from Schwitzer's." And, written just about thirty years in advance, there is also what might be taken as an amusing reference to this play — "drummatoysed by Mac Milligan's daughter" — (whose name, in the ballad referred to, happens to be Mary Ann). Taken separately, these odd evidences of pre-vision mean nothing at all, but taken collectively, they do give the impression that, like the Dead Sea Scrolls, *Finnegans Wake* has that upsetting quality of coming out too early, with far too much.

Another thing that Miss Manning seems to have tried to do is to bring out an element that is seldom touched upon, the fact that the *Wake* is an extremely funny book. Joyce was not often given the credit of being a humorist, a fact that he was heard to deplore on more than one occasion. The spirit of our times is inclined to be against laughter, particularly when matters of life and death are under discussion, and there are some who may reasonably object to the intrusion of so much of it into this version of so serious a work as the *Wake*. However, in the six hundred pages of the original there are many Sahara Deserts where those who hate the sight of a joke can refresh themselves with infinite vistas of dryness, and so I feel that here Miss Manning is doing Joyce a service in emphasizing the fact that he can be thoroughly enjoyed as well as parsed. Maybe that is why he paid her his graceful tribute, so far in advance.

From her record as a successful playwright and novelist with a considerable sense of humor, she is specially qualified to do this; while from her knowledge of Joyce's Dublin, and the background of all of his characters, she may be expected — in his own words — to wipe her glosses with what she knows. Not that it is necessarily a good thing to know too much about that slatternly seventh city of Christendom. Another of the peculiarities of the book is the fact that there is so much personal spite and malicious gossip half-concealed in its pages that many Dubliners allow themselves to be distracted by their natural annoyance over this from the tremendous qualities that the book also possesses.

The principal service, however, that Mary Manning performs for readers is, I think, in writing the stage directions. Most of us find that our greatest problem in making head or tail of *Finnegans Wake* lies in the difficulty of knowing who is talking at any particular moment, and to whom. Is it Shaun or Shem, Earwicker or Annie, the Four Masters (and which of them?) or Kate the scrubwoman, Joyce himself or the Father, the Son, or the Pidgeon? And to what extent does each character double up with the others, and if so, with which? For a work with such a multitude of names and overtones, there are surprisingly few people in the actual cast. They are largely the same numbers appearing and reappearing under different guises — Mutt, Jute, Justius, Mercius, Butt, Taff, Muta, Juva, Buckley, an unnamed Russian General, Persse O'Reilly, a mysterious Mr. Porter, Anna

Livia, the Prankquean, Iseult the leap-year girl, and that tiresome pair, Brown and Nolan, publishers of Nassau Street. It may be argued that so far there are only four people involved in this entire roll call.

Joyce always leaves us a text without any chapter heads, and in the *Wake* he goes even further and presents us with a play where, as in the Song of Solomon, we are expected to work out for ourselves who it is that is reporting or being reported in almost every line. The particular advantage in seeing even a small part of it performed upon the stage is that it solves so many of these problems for us, and allows us to enjoy the lines, without any preliminary roll call in order to find out who is present and who is not. All that is important is to be sure that the proper doubling is strictly observed by the casting department.

Everybody may not entirely agree with Miss Manning's solution of some of these questions, but if she is wrong in any of her interpretations, Joyce has nobody to blame except himself, and we have every cause to be grateful to Miss Manning for having seen us so far upon our way.

Better still is the fact that, having seen this dramatization upon the stage, or read it in this entertaining form, we should return posthaste to read the book itself, with a new sense both of its readability and of its importance.

D. J.

THE SCENES

Prologue to Everything

Scene One. The Fall

Scene Two. Resurrection

Scene Three. Anna Livia Plurabelle

Scene Four. The Tavern

Scene Five. The Dream Dramas

Scene Six. The End and the Beginning

THE CHARACTERS

Shem

Shaun

Anna Livia Plurabelle (ALP)

H. C. Earwicker-Finnegan

   and

   Eight members of the Chorus-Wake who

   play various roles

PROLOGUE TO EVERYTHING

The lights dim to a blackout. The percussion overture ends with a series of bangs and crashes of cymbals. Pause. From far away a horn blows reveille. Another pause, and the chorus speaks unseen.

CHORUS

riverrun, past Eve and Adam's, from swerve of shore to bend of bay, brings us by a commodius vicus of recirculation back to Howth Castle and Environs.

(*The horn blows again. This time much nearer.*)

RADIO ANNOUNCER

Silent. 566 A.D. At this time it fell out that a brazenlockt damsel grieved because that Puppette her minion was ravisht of her by the ogre Puropeus Pious. Bloody wars in Ballyaughacleeaghbally. 1132. A.D. Two sons at an hour were born until a goodman and his hag. These sons called themselves Caddy and Primas. Primas was a santryman and drilled all decent people. Caddy went to Winehouse and wrote o peace a farce. Blotty words for Dublin. (*Groans off from the chorus.*) Thus, too, for donkey's years. Year! Year! And laughtears! Back. Back. (*The percussion starts up again.*)

(*Whoosh, we're back in the Stone Age! Two travelers from the twentieth century seem to have jet-propelled themselves "by a commodius vicus of recirculation" into some haunt of primitive man. We hear sounds of banging and hammering and strange animal noises coming out of the darkness.*)

FIRST TRAVELER

(*A cultivated precise voice*) In the name of Anem this carl on the kopje in pelted thongs a parth a lone who the joebiggar be he? For-

I

shapen his pigmaid hoagshead, shroonk his plodsfoot. He hath locktoes, this shortshins. It is slaking nuncheon out of some thing's brain pan.

SECOND TRAVELER

(*The passionate pedant*) Me seemeth a dragon man.

FIRST TRAVELER

What a quhare soort of a mahan. It is evident the michindaddy.

SECOND TRAVELER

Cave! Scuse us, chorley guy! You tollerday donsk?

THE MICHINDADDY

N.

FIRST TRAVELER

You tolkatiff scowegian?

THE MICHINDADDY

Nn.

SECOND TRAVELER

You spigotty anglease?

THE MICHINDADDY

(*Angrily: he's an Irish michindaddy!*) Nnn.

FIRST TRAVELER

You phonio saxo?

THE MICHINDADDY

(*With rising rage*) Nnnn.

SECOND TRAVELER

(*Happily*) Clear all so! 'Tis a Jute. Let us swop hats and excheck a few strong verbs weak oach eather yapyazzard abast the blooty creeks.

(*The cavemen now take over. Two of them are fumbling for speech.*)

JUTE

(*A bright boy*) Yutah!

MUTT

(*A slow fellow*) Mukk's pleasurad.

JUTE

Are you jeff?

MUTT

Somehards.

JUTE

But you are not jeffmute?

MUTT

Noho. Only an utterer. (*He chokes.*)

JUTE

Whoa? Whoat is the mutter with you?

MUTT

(*Recovering himself*) I became a stun a stummer.

JUTE

(*Patronizingly*) What a hauhauhauhaudibble thing, to be cause! How, Mutt?

MUTT

Aput the buttle, surd.

JUTE

Whose poddle? Wherein?

MUTT

The Inns of Dungtarf where Used awe to be he.

JUTE

(*Insolently*) You that side your voise are almost inedible to me. (*Slapping sounds.*) Become a bitskin more wiseable, as if I were you.

3

MUTT

(*With rising rage*) Has? Has at? Hasatency? Urp, Boohooru! Booru Usurp! (*Heavy stamping.*) I trumple from rath in mine mines when I rimimirim! (*Sounds of violent combat.*)

JUTE

(*The victor*) One eyegonblack. Bisons is bisons. Let me fore all your hasitancy cross your qualm with trink gilt. Here have sylvan coyne, a piece of oak. (*They make it up amid cheers from the onlookers.*) Ghinees hies good for you. (*Noisy drinking and smacking of lips and much rude laughter. They fade out.*)

RADIO ANNOUNCER

(*Portentously*) Its world! It is the same told of all. Many. Miscegenations on miscegenations. They lived und laughed ant loved end left. (*Soft beating of the drum and his voice gradually fades.*) In the ignorance that implies impression that knits knowledge that finds the nameform that whets the wits that convey contacts that sweeten sensation that drives desire that adheres to attachment that dogs death that bitches birth that entails the ensuance of existentiality . . .

(*Clash of cymbals and we are rushed back through the ages to what can be roughly described as civilization — the first decade of the twentieth century in Ireland's capital city, Dublin.*)

4

SCENE ONE

Two male members of the Wake step out in front of the curtains and stand left and right stage. They are respectable citizens, wearing deep mourning. Slowly and solemnly they remove black gloves and bowler hats, and slowly and solemnly they address the audience.

FIRST DUBLINER

(*A pompous character*) Bygmester Finnegan, of the Stuttering Hand, freemen's maurer, lived in the broadest way immarginable in his rushlit toofarback for messuages before joshuan judges had given us numbers or Helviticus committed deuteronomy ... (*Applies handkerchief to eyes.*)

SECOND DUBLINER

(*A more sprightly person*) One yeastyday he sternely struxk his tete in a tub for to watsch the future of his fates but ere he swiftly stook it out again, by the might of moses, the very water was eviparated and all the guenneses had met their exodus so that ought to show you what a pentschanjeuchy chap he was!

(*Derisive laughter from chorus.*)

FIRST DUBLINER

During mighty odd years this man of hod, cement and edifices in Toper's Thorp piled buildung supra buildung pon the banks for the livers by the Soangso.

(*Cheers from chorus.*)

SECOND DUBLINER

He would caligulate by multiplicables the alltitude and malltitude until he seesaw by neatlight of the liquor wheretwin 'twas born, his

roundhead staple of other days to rise in undress maisonry up-
standed . . .

FIRST DUBLINER

(*Lifting hat reverently*) Joygrantit!

SECOND DUBLINER

(*Carried away by his own eloquence*) A waalworth of a skyerscape of
most eyeful hoyth entowerly, erigenating from next to nothing and
celescalating the himals and all, hierarchitectitiptitoploftical, with a
burning bush abob off its baubletop and with larrons o'toolers
clittering up and tombles a'buckets clottering down. (*Pauses ex-
hausted. Cheers from chorus revive him.*)

FIRST DUBLINER

(*Again lifts hat reverently*) Of the first was he to bare arms and a
name: Wassaily Booslaeugh of Riesengeborg. His crest of huroldry,
in vert with ancillars, troublant, argent, a hegoak, poursuivant,
horrid, horned. His scutschum fessed, with archers strung, helio, of
the second. Hootch is for husbandman handling his hoe.

(*Shocked screams from ladies of chorus.*)

CHORUS OF MEN

Hohohoho, Mister Finn, you're going to be Mister Finnagain! Come-
day morm and, O, you're vine! Sendday's eve and, ah, you're vine-
gar! Hahahaha, Mister Funn, you're going to be fined again!

(*Loud roll of drums.*)

SECOND DUBLINER

(*Anxious for gossip*) What brought about that tragoady thundersday
this municipal sin business?

FIRST DUBLINER

(*Pompous to the last*) Heed! It may half been a missfired brick, as
some say, or it mought have been due to a collupsus of his back
promises, as others looked at it, but his howd feeled heavy, his hoddit
did shake. (*Lifts hat reverently*) There was a wall of course in erec-

tion. (*Crash offstage*) Dimb! He stottered from the latter. (*Crash*) Damb! he was dud.

(*Groans from chorus.*)

BOTH DUBLINERS

(*In unison*) Mastabatoom, mastabadtomm, when a mon merries his lute is all long. For whole the world to see.

RADIO ANNOUNCER

Ilyam, Ilyum! The House of Atreox is fallen indeedust.

(*Horn off blows taps. The Dubliners put on their gloves. The horn blows again; this time it is a hunting horn.*)

CHORUS

(*Sadly*)
D'ye ken John Peel with his coat so gay,
He lived at Troutbeck once on a day,
But now he has gone far away, far away,
We shall ne'er hear his horn in the morning.

'Twas the sound of his horn brought me from my bed,
And the cry of his hounds which he oftimes led,
For Peel's "View Hallo!" would awaken the dead,
Or the fox from his lair in the morning.

FIRST DUBLINER

(*Sanctimoniously*) Omen, so sigh us.

SECOND DUBLINER

Only a fadograph of a yestern scene. He is smolten in our mist, woe-becanned and packt away. (*Cheerfully*) So that meal's dead off for summan, schlook, schlice and goodridhirring.

(*They put on their hats and sidle in behind the curtains just as the chorus breaks out into a rather drunken rendering of the first verse of "Finnegan's Wake."*)

CHORUS

Tim Finnegan lived in Walker Street.
A gentle Irishman, mighty odd,

He'd a beautiful brogue, so rich and sweet,
And to rise in the world he carried a hod,
But you see he'd a sort of a tippling way,
With a love for the liquor poor Tim was born,
And to help him through with his work each day
He'd a drop of the creature every morn.

Whack, hurrah! Blood and 'ounds!
Welt the flure, ye're trotters shake.
Isn't it the truth, I've tould ye?
Lots of fun at Finnegan's wake!

(*The curtain rises on the Wake. The setting consists of blue curtains, a cyclorama, and a platform backstage. The actors change the props; in fact the changes form part of the action. The coffin is, in every sense, dead center, feet downstage, head upstage; it is tilted and open, revealing the shrouded and unpredictable corpse of Finnegan. A L P, the widow, sits on the platform away from the other mourners. She is wearing a gray cloak with the hood half pulled over her face. Shem and Shaun, her sons, are seated downstage; Shaun stage right and Shem to the left. The other mourners are grouped around the coffin. Beside the widow is a small table containing bottles and glasses. The lighting is gloomy and subdued, with a ghastly spot on the corpse; the mourners are all wearing black. They are respectable middle-class persons, bordering, maybe, on the shabby genteel.*

Shem and Shaun, the brothers, show a family resemblance to each other, but they are very different characters. Shaun is more conventional, more organized, less sensitive than his brother. He is noisy and conceited whereas Shem is proud, lonely, and sad. They both have humor, but Shem has wit. Shem is angry and Shaun is mocking. Both brothers love to sing. Shem has a light tenor voice and Shaun is a baritone. The brothers lead the singing of the second verse.)

SHEM AND SHAUN

One morning Tim was rather full,
His head felt heavy and made him shake,
He fell from the ladder and broke his skull,
So they carried him home his corpse to wake;
They rolled him up in a nice clean sheet,
And laid him out upon the bed,

8

With fourteen candles around his feet
And a couple of dozen around his head.

CHORUS

Whack, hurrah! Blood and 'ounds!
Welt the flure, ye're trotters shake.
Isn't it the truth, I've tould ye?
Lots of fun at Finnegan's wake!
(*The song comes to a wild stamping and hand-clapping finale. There is a much-needed pause for breath.*)

FIRST WOMAN

(*A refined person*) So This Is Dyoublong?

SECOND WOMAN

(*Nervously, finger to lips*) Hush! Caution! Echoland!

THIRD WOMAN

How charmingly exquisite (*looking at corpse*).

CHORUS OF WOMEN

(*Bent over the coffin, keening to the corpse*) Macool, Macool, orra whyi deed ye diie? of a trying thirstay mournin? Sobs they sighdid at Fillagain's chrissormiss wake, all the hoolivans of the nation, prostrated in their consternation.

SECOND DUBLINER

(*Inspecting the corpse dispassionately*) He's stiff but he's steady is Priam Olim!

FIRST DUBLINER

(*Maudlin*) 'Twas he was the dacent gaylabouring youth.

THIRD DUBLINER

Sharpen his pillowscone, tap up his bier!

SECOND DUBLINER

With a bockalips of finisky fore his feet. And a barrowload of guenesis hoer his head. (*Sings*) Tee the tootal of the fluid hang the twoddle of the fuddled, O!

9

SHEM

(*Singing*)
Have you heard of one Humpty Dumpty
How he fell with a roll and a rumble
And curled up like Lord Olofa Crumple
By the butt of the Magazine Wall.

CHORUS

(*Singing*)
Of the Magazine Wall,
Hump, helmet and all?

SHAUN

(*Pointing at Shem*) Here comes that odious and still today insufficiently malestimated notesnatcher Shem the Penman.

(*Screams from ladies of chorus.*)

SHEM

(*Gesture to Shaun*) What a picture primitive! Shaun! Shaun! Post the post! Shaun in proper person stands before me. That young fellow looks the stuff, the Bel of Beaus' Walk, a prime card if ever was! Pep? No mistaking that beamish brow!

SHAUN

Shem is as short for Shemus as Jem is joky for Jacob. A few toughnecks are still getatable who pretend that aboriginally he was of respectable stemming but every honest to goodness man in the land of the space of today knows that his back life will not stand being written about in black and white.

(*Laughter.*)

SHEM AND SHAUN

(*Hands across the coffin*)
Three in one, one and three.
Shem and Shaun and the shame that sunders em.
Wisdom's son, folly's brother.

THIRD DUBLINER

(*Rises, addresses the corpse*) He dug in and dug out by the skill of his tilth for himself and all belonging to him and he sweated his crew beneath his auspice for the living, begad he did, our ancestor most worshipful. (*Sits.*)

ALP

(*Crying out*) And would again could whispring grassies wake him and may again when the fiery bird disembers . . . (*She hands out the glasses and bottles.*)

SHAUN

(*Taking over with great heartiness*) Grampupus is fallen down but grinny sprids the boord. (*He helps her to serve the drinks*) And will again if so be sooth by elder to his youngers shall be said. Have you whines for my wedding, did you bring bride and bedding, will you whoop for my deading is a?

CHORUS

(*Crescendo*) Wake! Wake! Wake! Wake! Wake! Usqueadbaugham! (*In the confusion they spill some of the whisky on the corpse. The corpse sits up.*)

CHORUS

(*In horror*) God save us!

FINNEGAN

(*Reproachfully*) Anam muck an dhoul! Did ye drink me doornail?

FIRST DUBLINER

(*Placating him*) Now be aisy, good Mr Finnimore, sir. And take your laysure like a god on pension and don't be walking abroad.

SECOND DUBLINER

Sure you'd only lose yourself in Healiopolis now and wet your feet maybe with the foggy dew's abroad.

THIRD DUBLINER

Meeting some sick old bankrupt or the Cottericks' donkey with his shoe hanging, or a slut snoring with an impure infant on a bench.

11

SECOND WOMAN

(*Sniffily*) 'Twould turn you against life, so 'twould.

THIRD WOMAN

And the weather's that mean too.

THIRD DUBLINER

You're better off, sir, where you are . . .

FINNEGAN

(*Sinking back*) Lord Allmarshy.

CHORUS

(*Soothingly*) Hep, hep, hurrah there! Hero! Seven times thereto we salute you! Drop in your tracks, babe! Be not unrested!

FINNEGAN

(*Faintly*) Load! So be yet!

CHORUS

(*With a sigh of relief they sit down*) News! News! News!

SHEM

(*Sardonically*) News? Everything's going on the same or so it appeals to all of us, in the old holmsted here.

SHAUN

Coughings all over the sanctuary, bad scrant to me aunt Florenza. The horn for breakfast, one o'gong for lunch and dinnerchime.

SHEM

(*In a Belfast dialect*) As popular as when Belly the First was keng and his members met in the Diet of Man.

SHAUN

The same shop slop in the window.

CHORUS

(*Shouting, crescendo*) News! News! News! All the news!

Meat took a drop when Reilly-Parsons failed.

SECOND DUBLINER

Coal's short but we've plenty of bog in the yard.

THIRD DUBLINER

And barley's up again, begrained to it.

FIRST DUBLINER

The lads is attending school nessans regular, sir.

SECOND DUBLINER

'Tisraely the truth!

THIRD DUBLINER

No isn't it, roman pathoricks?

FIRST WOMAN

Kevin's just a doat with his cherub cheek, chalking oghres on walls.

SECOND WOMAN

Hetty Jane's a child of Mary. She'll be coming (for they're sure to choose her) in her white of gold with a tourch of ivy to rekindle the flame on Felix Day.

THIRD WOMAN

(*Thoroughly warmed up*) But Essie Shanahan has let down her skirts. You remember Essie in our Luna's Convent? They called her Holly Merry her lips were so ruddyberry.

(*Drum off begins tapping a tango rhythm.*)

SECOND DUBLINER

(*Enthusiastically*) I'd poster those pouters on every jamb in the town.

THIRD DUBLINER

She's making her rep at Lanner's twicenightly.

13

THIRD WOMAN

(*Whirling into a dance*) With the tabarine tamtammers of the whirli-gigmagees.

SECOND DUBLINER

(*Admiringly*) Beats that cachucha flat.

THIRD DUBLINER

'Twould dilate your heart to go.

(*Finnegan, attracted by the dancing, unnoticed, begins to rise.*)

FIRST DUBLINER

(*Agonized*) Lookut.

(*There is bedlam when they all see the corpse!*)

SECOND DUBLINER

Aisy now, you decent man, with your knees and lie quiet and repose your honour's lordship!

THIRD DUBLINER

Hold him here, Ezekiel Irons, and may God strengthen you! (*The men force the reluctant corpse down.*)

SECOND DUBLINER

It's our warm spirits, boys, he's spooring.

FIRST DUBLINER

(*Gloomily*) Here's lumbos.

CHORUS

(*Imploringly*) Repose you now. Where misties swaddlum, where misches lodge none, where mystries pour kind on, O sleepy!

FINNEGAN

(*Down for good*) So be yet!

FIRST DUBLINER

(*Prophetlike*) There's already a big rody ram lad at random who will take your place. Humme the Cheapner, Esc, overseen as we thought him, yet a worthy of the naym . . .

H! C! E! (*Three drum beats.*)

CHORUS OF WOMEN

(*They face upstage, arms outstretched as if expecting someone, and as they speak the lights fade slowly*) . . . at this timecoloured place where we live in our paroqial fermament one tide on another, the twin turbane dhow, *The Bey for Dybbling*, this archipelago's first visiting schooner, with a wicklowpattern waxenwench at her prow for a figurehead, here comes our old offender, humile, commune and ensectuous from his nature, sober serious, he is ee and no counter he who will be ultimendly respunchable for the hubbub caused in Edenborough.

(*Light out. In this blackout the mourners solemnly parade around the coffin, joining in the chorus of the song sung by Shem and Shaun — "The Ballad of Persse O' Reilly." They mask the disappearance of the widow and Finnegan. The coffin lid is closed, and a plain green Irish flag draped across it.*)

SHEM AND SHAUN

(*Singing*)
Then we'll have a free trade Gaels' band and mass meeting
For to sod the brave son of Scandiknavery.
And we'll bury him down in Oxmanstown
Along with the devil and Danes.

CHORUS

(*Singing*)
With the deaf and dumb Danes,
And all their remains.

SHEM

(*Singing*)
And not all the king's men nor his horses
Will resurrect his corpus
For there's no true spell in Connacht or hell
(*bis*) That's able to raise a Cain.

(*The hunting horn again, but this time louder and with more cheer.*

15

The lights come up full and the whole stage is gay. Everyone faces backstage.)

CHORUS

(*Singing*)
'Twas the sound of his horn brought me from my bed,
And the cry of his hounds which he oftimes led,
For Peel's "View Halloo" would waken the dead,
Or the fox from his lair in the morning.

CHORUS

(*Shouting*) Our hero! Here Comes Everybody! (*A sweeping gesture upstage.*)

SCENE TWO

Finnegan, the late corpse, now enters resurrected into H. C. EAR-
WICKER, *accompanied by his wife* A L P. *He is a respectable citizen
with a slightly hunted look and a nervous stammer, very anxious to
please. He stands center back, facing the audience with his wife on his
arm and smiling apprehensively.*

CHORUS

(*Announcing Earwicker to the rhythm of* "*The House That Jack
Built*") . . . that large incorporate licensed vintner, such as he is,
from former times, nine hosts in himself, in his hydrocomic establishment and his ambling limfy peepingpartner, the slave of the ring
that worries the hand that sways the lamp that shadows the walk
that bends to his bane the busynext man that came on the cop with
the fenian's bark that pickled his widow that primed the pope that
passed it round on the volunteers' plate till it croppied the ears of
Purses Relle that kneed O'Connell up out of his doss that shouldered
Burke that butted O'Hara that woke the busker that grattaned his
crowd that bucked the jiggers to rhyme the rann that flooded the
routes in Eryan's isles from Malin to Clear and Carnsore Point to
Slynagollow and cleaned the pockets and ransomed the ribs of all
the listeners, leud and lay, that bought the ballad that Hosty made.

EARWICKER

(*Cheerfully*) Haveth Childers Everywhere. Shsh — shake, comeraid.
(*He shakes hands with the members of the Wake.*)

(*A L P sits in the background. The men of the chorus, sober faced,
hats off, sing the first verse of Moore's melody "Let Erin Remember."*)

17

(*Standing to attention, facing the audience*)
Let Erin remember the days of old
Ere her faithless sons betrayed her;
When Malachi wore the collar of gold,
Which he won from her proud invader;
When her kings, with standard of green unfurled,
Led the Red Branch knights to danger;
Ere the em'rald gem of the western world
Was set in the crown of a stranger.
(*They sit and all heads are bent in prayer.*)

SHEM

(*Every inch the young priest*) Let us pry.

CHORUS

(*Chanting*) Cur, quicquid, ubi, quando, quomodo, quoties quibus auxiliis?

SHEM

We thought, would and did. You were bred, fed, fostered and fattened from holy childhood up in this two easter island on the piejaw of hilarious heaven and roaring the other place (plunders to night of you, blunders what's left of you, flash as flash can!) and now, forsooth, a nogger among the blankards of this dastard century, condemned fool, anarch, egoarch, hiresiarch, you have reared your disunited kingdom on the vacuum of your own most intensely doubtful soul. Do you hold yourself then for some god in the manger, Shehohem, that you will neither serve not let serve, pray nor let pray?

(*The chorus rises. They turn their backs on Shem and surround Earwicker menacingly, derisively, as he stands down front.*)

SHEM

(*Bitterly*) Repopulate the land of your birth and count up your progeny by the hungered head and the angered thousand and thereby adding to the already unhappiness of this our popeyed world!

18

EARWICKER

(*Anxious to please everyone*) Sure it's all a question of pull. I believe in Dublin and the Sultan of Turkey.

FIRST DUBLINER

(*Pointing at him, derisively*) A baser meaning has been read into these characters the literal sense of which decency can safely scarcely hint. It has been blurtingly bruited by certain wisecrackers that he suffered from a vile disease.

THIRD WOMAN

(*Jumping up, violently*) None of your cumpohlstery English here!

SECOND WOMAN

(*Sniffing*) As to his religion, if any, it was the see-you-Sunday sort!

THIRD DUBLINER

Nor have his detractors, who, an imperfectly warmblooded race, mended their case by insinuating that, alternately, he lay at one time under the ludicrous imputation of annoying Welsh fusiliers in the people's park.

EARWICKER

I never —

CHORUS

(*Crescendo*) Hay, hay, hay! Hoq, hoq, hoq! (*They raise their right hands in a salute, surrounding the cowed Earwicker.*)

EARWICKER

(*Driven*) I am woowoo willing to take my stand, sir, upon the monument, that sign of our ruru redemption, any hygienic day to this hour and to make my hoath to my sinnfinners, even if I get life for it, upon the Open Bible and before the Great Taskmaster's (I lift my hat!) and in the presence of the Deity Itself andwell of Bishop and Mrs Michan of High Church of England as of all such of said my immediate withdwellers and of every living sohole in every corner wheresoever of this globe in general which useth of my British to my backbone tongue and commutative justice that there is not one tittle of truth, allow me to tell you, in that purest of fibfib fabrications.

THIRD DUBLINER

(*A big bully*) Lookut, will you come to the point?

SECOND WOMAN

(*Bawling to the world in general*) Now patience, and remember patience is a great thing and above all else we must avoid anything being, or becoming out of patience!

(*Laughter.*)

SECOND DUBLINER

(*Beside himself*) Keep it black! Keep it black!

SHAUN

(*Pointing at Shem*) Sniffer of carrion, premature gravedigger, seeker of the nest of evil in the bosom of a good word, you, who sleep at our vigil and fast for our feast, you with your dislocated reason, have cutely foretold, a jophet in your own absence, by blind poring upon your many scalds and burns and blisters, by the auspices of that raven cloud, your shade, and by the auguries of rooks in parlament, death with every disaster, the dynamitisation of colleagues, the reducing of records to ashes, the levelling of all customs by blazes, the return of a lot of sweetempered gunpowdered didst unto dudst but it never stphruck your mudhead's obtundity. (*Shem, laughing, moves up to him, stands the other side of Earwicker*) O hell, here comes our funeral! O pest, I'll miss the post! that the more carrots you chop, the more turnips you slit, the more murphies you peel, the more onions you cry over, the more bullbeef you butch, the more mutton you crackerhack, the more potherbs you pound, the fiercer the fire and the longer your spoon and the harder you gruel with more grease to your elbow the merrier fumes your new Irish stew.

(*Cheers and groans from chorus.*)

SHAUN

(*Mocking Earwicker*) Let me finish! Just a little judas tonic, my ghem of all jokes, to make you go green in the gazer. Do you hear what

I'm seeing, hammet? And remember that golden silence gives consent, Mr Anklegazer! Cease to be civil, learn to say nay! Whisht! (*He moves to Shem*) Come here, Herr Studiosus, till I tell you a wig in your ear. We'll do a whisper drive, for if the barishnyas got a twitter of it they'd tell the housetops. It's secret! (*The chorus begins whispering amongst themselves*) I had it from Lamppost Shawe. And Rantipoll tipped the wink from old Mrs Tinbullet. And as for she was confussed by pro-Brother Thacolicus. And the good brother feels he would need to defecate you. And Kelly, Kenny and Keogh are up up and in arms. That a cross may crush me if I refuse to believe in it. That I may rock anchor through the ages if I hope it's not true. Sh! Shem, you are. Sh! You are mad!

CHORUS

He points the deathbone and the quick are still. *Insomnia, somnia somniorum. Awmawm.*

SHEM

(*Defiantly*) *Domine vopiscus!* My fault, his fault, a kingship through a fault! Pariah, cannibal Cain, I who oathily forswore the womb that bore you and the paps I sometimes sucked, you who ever since have been one black mass of jigs and jimjams, haunted by a convulsionary sense of not having been or being all that I might have been or you meant to becoming, bewailing like a man that innocence which I could not defend like a woman, lo you there, Cathmon-Carbery, and thank Movies from the innermost depths of my still attrite heart Wherein the days of youyouth are evermixed mimine, now ere the compline hour of being alone athands itself and a puff or so before we yield our spiritus to the wind . . . it is to you, firstborn and firstfruit of woe, to me, branded sheep, pick of the wasterpaperbaskel, you alone, windblasted tree of the knowledge of beautiful andevil, to me unseen blusher in an obscene coalhole, the cubilibum of your secret sigh, dweller in the downandoutermost where voice only of the dead may come, because ye left from me, because ye laughed on me, because . . .

ALP

O me lonly son, ye are forgetting me! (*She comes towards him.*)

21

(*Softly*) Beside the rivering waters of, hitherandthithering waters of . . . Anna Livia Plurabelle, that our turfbrown mummy is acoming, alpilla, beltilla, ciltilla, deltilla, running with her tidings, old the news of the great big world.

ALP

(*Beside Shem*) O me lonly son, ye are forgetting me! (*Shem faces her. She moves away from him smiling and ascends the platform.*)

CHORUS

(*Turning upstage to her as the lights fade*) With a beck, with a spring, all her rillringlets shaking, rocks drops in her tachie, tramtokens in her hair, all waived to a point and then all inuendation, little old-fashioned mummy, little wonderful mummy, ducking under bridges, bellhopping the weirs, dodging by a bit of bog, rapid-shooting round the bends, by Tallaght's green hills and the pools of the phooka and a place they call it Blessington and slipping sly by Sally-noggin, as happy as the day is wet, babbling, bubbling, chattering to herself, deloothering the fields on their elbows leaning with the sloothering slide of her, giddygaddy, grannyma, gossipaceous Anna Livia.

(*Lights go down and chorus exits. There is one spot on Shem singing the sad song of "The Exile of Erin."*)

SHEM

There came to the beach a poor exile of Erin,
The dew on his robes was heavy and chill;
For his country he sighed when at twilight repairing,
To wander alone by the wind-beaten hill.
But the day star attracted his eye's sad devotion,
For it rose on its own native isle of the ocean,
Where once on the flow of his youthful emotion,
He sang the bold anthem of Erin go bragh.

(*The spot moves to Shaun.*)

SHAUN

(*Sings jeeringly to the same tune*)
If you met on the binge a poor acheseyeld from Ailing,

When the tune of his tremble shook shimmy on shin,
While his countrary raged in the weak of his wailing,
Like a rugilant pugilant Lyon O'Lynn;
If he weapt while he leapt and guffalled quith a quhimper,
Made cold blook a blue mundy and no bones without flech,
Taking kiss, kake or kick with a suck, sigh or simper,
A diffle to larn and a dibble to lech;
If the fain shinner pegged you to shave his immartial,
Wee skillmustered shoul with his ooh, hoodoodoo!
Broking wind that to wiles, woemaid sin he was partial,
We don't think, Jones, we'd care to this evening, would you?

*(He lifts his hat in a salute and saunters out. The dim figures of two
washerwomen and a chorus of two other women move into view and
take up their positions; the washerwomen stand on the platform and the
chorus seat themselves on the coffin, one woman on either end with her
back to the other. The spot is now on Shem, who continues to sing as
if he were alone.)*

SHEM

Erin, my country, though sad and forsaken,
In dreams I revisit thy sea-beaten shore;
But alas, in a far foreign land I awaken,
And sigh for the friends who can meet me no more.
O cruel fate, wilt thou never replace me
In a mansion of peace — where no perils can chase me?
Never again shall my brothers embrace me?
They died to defend me or live to deplore.
(As he moves away he sings the first four lines of the last verse.)
Yet with all its sad recollections suppressing,
One dying wish my lone bosom can draw;
Erin, an exile bequeaths thee his blessing,
Land of my forefathers, Erin go bragh!
(His voice dies away in the distance.)

SCENE THREE

It is late afternoon in summer and the two women are washing clothes in the Liffey. They wear kerchiefs and aprons over their wake clothes. The chorus is played by two women in dark cloaks. Their speeches reflect the sounds of the ducks, the wind in the reeds, the lapping of the water, and so forth.

A VOICE

(*Calls loudly*) He lifts the lifewand and the dumb speak.

CHORUS

(*The ducks quacking in the reeds*) Quoiquoiquoiquoiquoiquoiquoiq!

FIRST WOMAN

(*A big earthy creature*) Anna Livia . . . (*she calls across the river*).

SECOND WOMAN

(*She is small, cross, and sharp*) Anna Livia . . .

CHORUS

Anna Livia. Tell me all about Anna Livia. I want to hear all about Anna Livia.

FIRST WOMAN

Well, you know Anna Livia?

SECOND WOMAN

Yes, of course, we all know Anna Livia. Tell me all. Tell me now.

24

FIRST WOMAN

You'll die when you hear. (*The chorus laughs.*) Well, you know, when the old cheb went futt and did what you know.

CHORUS

Hush. Hush. Hush. Hush.

SECOND WOMAN

Yes, I know, go on. Wash quit and don't be dabbling. Tuck up your sleeves and loosen your talktapes. And don't butt me — hike! — when you bend.

FIRST WOMAN

Whatever it was they threed to make out he thried to two in the Fiendish park.

CHORUS

(*Scandalized*) Tush! Tush! Tush! Tush!

FIRST WOMAN

He's an awful old reppe. Look at the shirt of him! Look at the dirt of it! He has all my water black on me. The duddurty devil! Scorching my hand and starving my famine to make his private linen public.

SECOND WOMAN

And how long was he under loch and neagh?

FIRST WOMAN

It was put in the newses what he did.

SECOND WOMAN

O, the roughty old rappe! Minxing marrage and making loof. Tell me all. Tell me more . . .

CHORUS

Vuggybarney, Wickermandy! Hello, ducky, please don't die! Quoi-quoiquoiquoiquoi!

FIRST WOMAN

Shyr she's nearly as badher as him herself.

Who? Anna Livia?

Anna Livia. Do you know she was calling bakvandets sals from all around to go in till him, her erring cheef, and tickle the pontiff aisy-oisy?

WhoooooWhooooo . . .

(*Delightedly*) O botlettle I thought she'd act that loa!

Calling them in, one by one and legging a jig or so on the sihl to show them how to shake their benders and the dainty how to bring to mind the gladdest garments out of sight and all the way of a maid with a man and making a sort of a cackling noise like two and a penny or half a crown and holding up a silliver shiner.

Lordy, lordy, did she so? Well, of all the ones ever I heard! Throwing all the neiss little whores in the world at him! I'm dying down off my iodine feet until I lerryn Anna Livia's cushingloo, that was writ by one and rede by two and trouved by a poule in the parco!

Listen now. Are you listening?

Yes, yes! Idneed I am!

By earth and the cloudy but I badly want a brandnew bankside, bedamp and I do, and a plumper at that! For the putty affair I have is wore out, so it is, sitting, yaping and waiting for my old Dane hodder dodderer, my life in death companion, my frugal key of our larder, my much-altered camel's hump, my jointspoiler, my may-moon's honey, my fool to the last Decemberer, to wake himself out of his winter's doze and bore me down like he used to.

FIRST WOMAN

She was just a young thin pale soft shy slim slip of a thing then, sauntering, by silvamoonlake and he was a heavy trudging lurching lieabroad of a Curraghman, making his hay for whose sun to shine on, as tough as the oaktrees (peats be with them!) used to rustle that time down by the dykes of killing Kildare, for forstfellfoss with a plash across her. She thought she's sankh neathe the ground with nymphant shame when he gave her the tigris eye!

SECOND WOMAN

(*With infinite relish*) O happy fault! Me wish it was he!

FIRST WOMAN

(*Reprovingly*) You're wrong there, corribly wrong! Tisn't only tonight you're anacheronistic! It was ages behind that when nullahs were nowhere, in county Wickenlow, garden of Erin . . .

CHORUS

(*In great excitement*) Neya, narev, nen, nonni, nos! Then where-abouts in Ow and Ovoca? Was it yst with wyst or Lucan Yokan or where the hand of man has never set foot? Dell me where, the fairy ferse time!

FIRST WOMAN

(*Irritated*) I will if you listen. You know the dinkel dale of Lugge-law? Well, there once dwelt a local heremite, Michael Arklow was his riverend name, (with many a sigh I aspersed his lavabibs!) and one venersderg in junojuly, oso sweet and so cool and so limber she looked, Nance the Nixie, Nanon L'Escaut, in the silence, of the sycomores, all listening, the kindling curves you simply can't stop feeling, he plunged both of his newly anointed hands, the core of his cushlas, in her singimari saffron strumans of hair, parting them and soothing her and mingling it, that was deepdark and ample like this red bog at sundown.

27

By that Vale Vowclose's lucydlac, the reignbeau's heavenarches
arronged orranged her. Wish a wish! Why a why? Mavro! Letty
Lerck's lafing light throw those laurals now on her daphdaph tease-
song petrock. Maass!

FIRST WOMAN

But first of all, worst of all, the wiggly livvly, she sideslipped out
by a gap in the Devil's glen while Sally her nurse was sound asleep
in a sloot and, feefee fiefie, fell over a spillway before she found her
stride and lay and wriggled in all the stagnant black pools of rainy
under a fallow coo and she laughed innocefree with her limbs aloft
and a whole drove of maiden hawthorns blushing and looking
askance upon her.

SECOND WOMAN

(*Hungry for more*) Drop me the sound of the findhorn's name, Mtu
or Mti, sombogger was wisness. And drip me why in the flenders
was she frickled. Are you in the swim or are you out? O go in, go
on, go an! I mean about what you know.

FIRST WOMAN

I know right well what you mean. Rother! You'd like the coifs and
guimpes, snouty, and me to do the greasy jub on old Veronica's
wipers. What am I rancing now and I'll thank you? Is it a pinny or
is it a surplice?

SECOND WOMAN

Arran, where's your nose? And where's the starch? O, may the
diabolo twisk your seifety pin! You child of Mammon, Kinsella's
Lilith! Now who has been tearing the leg of her drawars on her?

FIRST WOMAN

(*With dreadful interest*) Which leg is it?

SECOND WOMAN

The one with the bells on it.

FIRST WOMAN

Rinse them out and aston along with you! Where did I stop?

SECOND WOMAN

Never stop. Continuarration! You're not there yet. I amstel waiting. Garonne, garonne!

FIRST WOMAN

So she said to herself she'd frame a plan to fake a shine, the mischief-maker, the like of it you niever heard.

SECOND WOMAN

What plan? What the meurther did she mague?

FIRST WOMAN

Well, she bergened a zakbag, a shammy mailsack, with the lend of a loan of the light of his lampion, off one of her swapsons, Shaun the Post, and then she went and consulted her chapboucqs, old Mot Moore, Casey's Euclid and the Fashion Display and made herself tidal to join in the mascarete. (*Convulsed with laughter*) O gig goggle of gigguels. I can't tell you how!

CHORUS

Minneha, minnehi minaaehe, minneho!

SECOND WOMAN

O but you must, you must really! By the holy well of Mulhuddart I swear I'd pledge my chanza getting to heaven through Tirry and Killy's mount of impiety to hear it all, aviary word.

FIRST WOMAN

O, leave me my faculties, woman, a while! If you don't like my story get out of the punt.

SECOND WOMAN

Well, have it your own way, so. Tongue your time now. Breathe thet deep. Lynd us your blessed ashes here till I scrub the canon's underpants. Flow now . . .

FIRST WOMAN

She wove a garland for her hair. She pleated it. She plaited it. Of meadowgrass and riverflags, the bulrush and waterweed, and of fallen griefs of weeping willow. She said she wouldn't be half her length away. Then, then, as soon as the lump his back was turned, with her mealiebag slang over her shulder, Anna Livia, oysterface, forth of her bassein came.

CHORUS

Wish a whish a wish a wish.

SECOND WOMAN

Describe her! Hustle along, why can't you? Spitz on the iern while it's hot. What had she on, the liddel oud oddity?

FIRST WOMAN

Will you hold your peace and listen well to what I am going to say now? It might have been ten or twenty to one of the night of Allclose or the nexth of April when the flip of her hoogly igloo flappered and out toetippit a bushman woman, the dearest little moma ever you saw, nodding around her, all smiles. She wore a ploughboy's nail-studded clogs, a pair of ploughfields in themselves: a sugarloaf hat with a gaudyquiviry peak and a band of gorse for an arnoment: her nude cuba stockings were salmospotspeckled: stout stays, the rivals, lined her length: her bloodorange bockknickers, a two in one garment, showed natural nigger boggers, fancyfastened, free to undo: she had a clothespeg tight astride on her joki's nose and she kep on grinding a sommething quaint in her fiumy mouth and her snuffdrab siouler's skirt trailed ffifty odd Irish miles behind her lungarhodes.

SECOND WOMAN

Hellsbells, I'm sorry I missed her! Sweet gumptyum and nobody fainted!

FIRST WOMAN

(*With infinite calm*) Everyone that saw her said the dowce little delia looked a bit queer. And they crowned her their chariton queen, all the maids.

SECOND WOMAN

Of the may? You don't say! My colonial, wardha bagful! That's what you may call a tale of a tub. You've all the swirls your side of the current.

Well, am I to blame for that if I have? You're a bit on the sharp side. I'm on the wide. (*The Angelus rings faintly in the distance. The voices of the women become more lyrical.*) Well, you know or don't you kennet or haven't I told you every telling has a taling and that's the he and the she of it.

SECOND WOMAN

Look, look, the dusk is growing.

FIRST WOMAN

My branches lofty are taking root (*she slowly raises her arms*) and my cold cher's gone ashley. Fieluhr? Filou! What age is at?

SECOND WOMAN

It saon is late. O, my back, my back, my bach! I'd want to go to Aches-les-Pains. Pingpong! (*The bell rings nearer now.*) There's the Belle for Sexaloitez! And Concepta de Send-us-pray! Pang!

FIRST WOMAN

Pong! Wring out the clothes! Wring in the dew! Godavari, vert the showers!

SECOND WOMAN

And grant thaya grace! Aman.

FIRST WOMAN

Will we spread them here now?

SECOND WOMAN

Ay, we will. Flip! Spread on your bank and I'll spread mine on mine. It's churning chill . . .

FIRST WOMAN

Flep! It's what I'm doing. Spread! Der went is rising. I'll lay a few stones on the hostel sheets. A man and his bride embraced between them. Else I'd have sprinkled and folded them only.

31

Throw the cobwebs from your eyes, woman, and spread your washing proper! It's well I know your sort of slop. Flap! Ireland sober is Ireland stiff. Lord help you, Maria, full of grease, the load is with me!

FIRST WOMAN

(*Dreamily. She is now the elm*) Ah, but she was the queer old skeowsha anyhow, Anna Livia, trinkettoes! And sure he was the quare old buntz too, Dear Dirty Dumpling, foostherfather of fingalls and dotthergills. Gammer and gaffer we're all their gangsters.

(*Lights begin fading.*)

SECOND WOMAN

The seim anew. Ordovico or viricordo. Anna was, Livia is, Plurabelle's to be.

CHORUS

Can't hear with the waters of. The chittering waters of. Flittering bats, fieldmice bawk talk.

FIRST WOMAN

(*Calling across the river*) Ho! Are you not gone ahome?

SECOND WOMAN

(*Dimly*) What Thom Malone? (*She is now the stone.*)

CHORUS

(*Urgently*) Can't hear with bawk of bats, all thim liffeying waters of. Ho, talk save us!

SECOND WOMAN

(*Looking up from her huddled position at the other, who, with arms upraised, is now forever the tree*) My foos won't moos. I feel as old as yonder elm.

CHORUS

A tale told of Shaun or Shem? All Livia's daughtersons. Dark hawks hear us. Night! Night! My ho head halls. I feel as heavy as yonder stone. Tell me of John or Shaun? Who were Shem and Shaun the living sons or daughters of? Night now! Tell me, tell me, tell me, elm! Night night! Telmetale of stem or stone. Beside the rivering waters of, hitherandthithering waters of. Night!

(Darkness. Nothing is heard but the bell ringing the Angelus, and then it too fades into the distance.)

SCENE FOUR

The lights come up to the sound of roaring, discordant, drunken singing.

CHORUS

My wife and I live all alone,
In a little brown hut we call our own;
She loves gin and I love rum,
Tell you what, don't we have fun!

Ha, ha, ha, you and me,
Little brown jug, don't I love thee?
Ha, ha, ha, you and me,
Little brown jug, how I love thee!

It is closing time in Mr. Earwicker's licensed establishment. The hero himself, in his shirt sleeves and wearing an apron, is swaying in the door ringing a hand bell. A "dreary cowery lad," the potboy, is pushing a wet mop across the floor and watching his employer's peregrinations with some apprehension.

CHORUS

(*Men, offstage*) Nine hosts in himself, in his hydrocomic establishment and his ambling limfy peepingpartner, the slave of the ring that worries the hand that sways the lamp that shadows the walk that bends to his bane the busynext man and cleaned the pockets and ransomed the ribs of all the listeners, leud and lay, that bought the ballad that Hosty made.

EARWICKER

Time, gentlemen. Dang! Ding! Dong! Dung! Dinnin! (*He staggers out through the door and the singing dies away.*)

34

POTBOY

(*Singing*)
I dreamt that I dwelt in marble halls,
With vassals and serfs at my side . . .

(*He goes on and on like a broken record. Presently Earwicker returns between Shem and Shaun, who both manage to keep him upright, though they are very drunk themselves.*)

SHAUN

(*Indicating the hero*) So poor old hospitable corn and eggfactor, King Roderick O'Conor, the paramount chief polemarch and last pre-electric king of Ireland, who was anything you say yourself between fiftyodd and fiftyeven years of age at the time after the socalled last supper he greatly gave in his umbrageous house of the hundred bottles with the radio beamer tower and its hangars . . .

SHEM

(*Fuddled*) Or, at least, he wasn't actually the then last king of all Ireland . . .

EARWICKER

(*Frees himself*) So you were saying, boys? (*He drones to the tune of the "Little Brown Jug"*) For be all rules of sport 'tis right That youth bedower'd to charm the night Whilst age is dumped to mind the day When wather parted from the say. (*He staggers around, followed by the anxious potboy*) High! Sink! High! Sink! Highhohigh! Sinkasink! (*He sinks; the potboy catches him*) Waves!

POTBOY

(*In pallid despair*) Oh dere! Ah hoy!

SHAUN

Wait till I tell you, what did he do, poor old Roderick O'Conor Rex, the auspicious waterproof monarch of all Ireland, when he found himself all alone by himself in his grand old handwedown pile . . . (*He breaks into song and is immediately joined by Earwicker, Shem, and the potboy.*)

35

Alone, all alone, by the wave-washed strand,
And alone in the crowded hall.
The hall it is gay and the waves are grand,
But my heart is not there at all.
It flies far away, by night and by day,
To the time and the place that are gone.
O I never can forget the sweet colleen I met
In the valley near Slievenamon.

EARWICKER

(*Bursting into tears*) Alone, all alone, so you were saying, boys? Anyhow he what?

SHAUN

What did he do, poor old Roderick O'Conor Rex (*making an effort*) after all of them had all gone off with themselves to their castles of mud, as best they cud, on footback, owing to the leak of the McCarthy's mare, in extended order . . .

EARWICKER

(*Reeling around the coffin, as if to tidy up, airily*) I've a terrible errible lot todue todie todue tootorribleday. (*He slumps across the coffin to the roll and thump of drums offstage.*)

POTBOY

O boy, you're troo!

(*The three of them reverently lay out the body, arms crossed, with the flag across it, and then slowly march around it, the potboy ringing the hand bell, as a server at the Mass, after each line.*)

SHAUN AND SHEM

(*Intoning*)
Mattheehew, Markeehew, Lukeehew, Johnheehewwheehew!
Haw!
And still a light moves long the river. And stiller the mermen ply their keg.

Its pith is full. The way is free. Their lot is cast.
So, to john for a john, johnajeams, led it be!

CHORUS

(*Gregorian chant, far away*) Now follow we out by Starloe! He dreams his dreams.

(*The coffin is now a ship, the ship which is to bear the hero and Iseult to Cornwall and King Mark. The potboy hoists the wet mop as a mast, his apron makes a sail, one string tied to the mop-mast, the other around Earwicker's toe. Shaun and the potboy place themselves on either side of it as sailors at attention. Shem, carrying the hand bell, leaps on to the coffin-bow, hand to brow, scanning the horizon. A L P enters wearing a red wig circled by a wreath of gold leaves, flowing green garments, and carrying a gold harp. She places herself in a for- ward-leaning stance at the coffin-prow, harp outstretched, and becomes the figurehead.*)

CHORUS

(*Women's voices, chanting nearer*) Now follow we out by Starloe! He dreams his dreams.

ALP

(*Intoning*) Overhoved, shrillgleescreaming. That song sang sea- swans. The winging ones. Seahawk, seagull, curlew and plover, kestrel and capercallzie. All the birds of the sea . . .

SHEM

(*Shouting commands to the crew and ringing the bell*) Heave hone, leave lone, Larry's on the focse and Faugh MacHugh O'Bawlar at the wheel, one to do (*Shaun kneels*), and one to dare (*potboy kneels*), par by par, a peerless pair, ever here and over there . . .

(*The lights begin to fade, Shaun and the potboy pull on the imaginary oars in unison.*)

SHEM, SHAUN, AND POTBOY

(*As if singing a chantey*) With his fol the dee oll the doo on the flure of his feats and the feels of the fumes in the wakes of his ears . . .

37

SHEM

(*Scanning the horizon*) So sailed the stout ship *Nansy Hans*. From Liff away. For Nattenlaender. As who has come returns. (*He waves back to shore*) Farvel, farerne! Goodbark, goodbye!

WOMEN'S VOICES

Now follow we out by Starloe! He dreams his dreams.

(*Darkness. Sound of seagulls. Music swells as the scene ends.*)

SCENE FIVE

Music. The lights rise slowly revealing Earwicker still unconscious on the coffin, which now stands on a platform upstage. Below it, the woman (A L P) is seated, twanging on the harp. The music fades on some muted twanging.

ALP

(*Wailing*) Lowly, longly, a wail went forth. Pure Yawn lay low. (*Women wail obediently backstage.*) On the mead of the hillock lay, heartsoul dormant mid shadowed landshape, brief wallet to his side, and arm loose, by his staff of citron briar, tradition stick-pass-on. (*More wailing.*)

(Shaun and Shem enter right and left. They wear straw boaters, tennis flannels, colorful blazers, and carry walking sticks.)

SHAUN

(*Indicating the harpist*) History as her is harped!

SHEM

(*Inspecting the sleeping Earwicker, who is muttering, groaning, and snoring*) Most distressfully (but, my dear, how successfully!) to wail he did, his locks of a lucan tinge, quickrich, ripely rippling, unfilleted, those lashbetasselled lids on the verge of closing time, whiles ouze of his sidewiseopen mouth the breath of him (*a snore*)! Yawn in a semiswoon lay awailing . . . His dream monologue was over, of cause, but his drama parapolylogic had yet to be, affact.

(There is a clash of cymbals, the lights flash, and a roll of drums follows. A voice offstage bellows: "Silence!")

39

SHAUN

(*Confronting A L P, who has risen in great indignation*) A space. Who are you?

ALP

(*Majestically*) The cat's mother. A time.

SHAUN

What do you lack?

ALP

The look of a queen! (*She sweeps past them and out, intoning*) She shall be dismembered forever, they shall be dismembered forever . . .

SHEM

(*Calling after her derisively*) Kate the Crone! Kothereen the Slop! Cacklin', no foolering! . . .

(*There is a roll of drums and a blackout.*)

VOICES

(*Offstage*)
— Act drop.
— Stand by!
— Blinders!
— Curtain up.
— Juice, please!
— Foots!

RADIO ANNOUNCER

We are now in the magnetic field! Moisten your lips for a lightning strike and begin again! I repeat, We are now in the Dream Place . . .

(*The ballet music begins, and the lights rise. Shaun moves down right and Shem seats himself just below the coffin. Shaun is wearing a professor's gown and is drinking from a bottle.*)

SHEM

Song! Shaun, song! Have mood! Hold forth!

(*Chokes*) I apologuise. (*He hands the bottle to Shem, who receives it gratefully. Shaun now becomes the Professor.*) I would rather spinooze you one from the grimm gests of Jacko and Esaup, fable one, feeble too. Let us here consider the casus, my dear little cousis of the Ondt and the Gracehoper.

(*The dancers run on and take up their positions. The Ondt and the Gracehoper are made up to resemble Shaun and Shem. The four ladies are of course highly stylized little insects — a flea, a louse, a bee, and a wasp.*)

SHAUN

The Gracehoper was always jigging ajog, hoppy on akkant of his joyicity, or, if not, he was always making ungraceful overtures to Floh and Luse and Bienie and Vespatilla to play pupa-pupa and pulicy-pulicy and to commence insects with him. A high old tide for the barheated publics and the whole day as gratiis! Fudder and lighting for ally looty, any filly in a fog.

Grouscious me and scarab my sahul! What a bagateller it is! Libelulous! Inzanzarity! Pou! Pschla! Ptuh! What a zeit for the goths! vented the Ondt, who, not being a sommerfool, was thothfolly making chilly spaces at hisphex affront of the icinglass of his windhame, which was cold antitopically Nixnixundnix. We shall not come to party at that lopp's, he decided possibly, for he is not on our social list.

The Ondt was a weltall fellow, raumybult and abelboobied. He was sair sair sullemn and chairmanlooking when he was not making spaces in his psyche, but, laus! when he wore making spaces on his ikey, he ware mouche mothst secred and muravyingly wisechairmanlooking. Now whim the sillybilly of a Gracehoper had jingled through a jungle of love and debts and jangled through a jumble of life in doubts afterworse, wetting with the bimblebeaks, drikking with nautonects, bilking with durrydunglecks and horing after ladybirdies (*ichnehmon diagelegenaitoikon*) he fell joust as sieck as a sexton. O moy Bog, he contrited with melanctholy. Meblizzered, him sluggered! I am heartily hungry!

He had eaten all the whilepaper, swallowed the lustres, devoured forty flights of styearcases, but when Chrysalmas was on the bare branches, off he went from Tingsomingenting. He took a round stroll and he took a stroll round and he took a round strollagain till the grillies in his head and the leivnits in his hair made him thought he had the Tossmania. Was he come to hevre with his engiles or gone to hull with the poop? Graussssssss! Opr! Graussssssss! Opr!

Behailed His Gross the Ondt, prostrandvorous upon his dhrone, in his Papylonian babooshkees, smolking a spatial brunt of Hosana cigals, with unshrinkables farfalling from his unthinkables, swarming of himself in his sunnyroom, sated before his comfortumble phullup-suppy of a plate o'monkynous and a confucion of minthe (for he was a conformed aceticist and aristotaller), as appi as a oneysucker or a baskerboy on the Libido, with Floh biting his leg thigh and Luse lugging his luff leg and Bieni bussing him under his bonnet and Vespatilla blowing cosy fond tutties up the allabroad length of the large of his smalls. As entomate as intimate could pinchably be. Emmet and demmet and be jiltses crazed and be jadeses whipt! schneezed the Gracehoper.

The Ondt, that true and perfect host, was making the greatest spass a body could with his queens laceswinging for he was spizzing all over him like thingsumanything in formicolation, boundlessly blissfilled in an allallahbath of houris. Chasing Floh out of charity and tickling Luse, I hope too, and tackling Bienie, faith, as well, and jucking Vespatilla jukely by the chimiche. Never did Dorsan from Dunshanagan dance it with more devilry! The veripatetic imago of the impossible Gracehoper on his odderkop in the myre, actually and presumptuably sinctifying chronic's despair, was sufficiently and probably coocoo much for his chorous of gravitates. (*Here he bursts into song, sympathetically accompanied by Shem, to the tune of* "*Yankee Doodle.*") Flunkey Footle furloughed foul, writing off his phoney, but Conte Carme makes the melody that mints the money.

SHEM

(*Joining him, and turning out his empty pockets*) Ad majorem l.s.d.! Divi gloriam. A darkener of the threshold.

SHAUN

(*Disgustedly*) Haru? Be it! So be it! Thou-who-thou-art, the fleet-as-sprindhrift, impfang thee of mine wideheight. Haru!

(*The dancers vanish and the two take center like a pair of music-hall comedians.*)

The thing pleased him andt, and andt,
He larved ond he larved on he merd such a nauses
The Gracehoper feared he would mixplace his fauces.
(*Tearfully*) I forgive you, grondt Ondt, said the Gracehoper, weep-
    ing,
For their sukes of the sakes you are safe in whose keeping.
Your feats end enormous, your volumes immense,
(May the Graces I hoped for sing your Ondtship song sense!),
Your genus its worldwide, your spacest sublime!
But, Holy Saltmartin, why can't you beat time?

SHEM AND SHAUN

In the name of the former and of the latter and of their holocaust.
Allmen.

(*The lights begin fading. Earwicker sits up.*)

EARWICKER

(*Aroused from dream*) Where are we at all? And whenabouts in the
name of space?

(*Blackout.*)

CONFUSION OF VOICES OVER THE RADIO

— Is that yu, Whitehed?
— Have you headnoise now?
— Give us your mespilt reception, will yous?
— Will you give me trunks, miss? Johnny MacDougal speaking . . .
— Pass the fish for Christ's sake!
— Pity poor Haveth Childers Everywhere.

EARWICKER

(*Shouting like one in a nightmare*) Till daybowbreak and show-
shadows flee. Thus be hek. Verily! Verily!

RADIO ANNOUNCER

Hear, O hear, Iseult la belle! Tristan, sad hero, hear!

(*Music. Wagnerian echoes from "Tristan and Isolda." The lights
come up, and A L P sits, in the character of Iseult and wearing her*

43

widow's weeds, just below the coffin. She is weeping. Shaun and Shem stand as sentinels on either side of her.)

WOMEN'S VOICES (*off*)

(*Echoes of the Rhine maidens*) Among the shivering sedges so. Hoo-hoo hoo! Hoohoo hoo! Weedy waving. Or tulipbeds of Rush below. Hoohoo hoo! Besides the bubblye waters of. The rivering waters of, the hitherandthithering waters of. Hoo, whoo, hoo, hoo (*they fade out*).

SHAUN

Poor Isa sits a glooming so gleaming in the gloaming; the tincelles a touch tarnished wind no lovelinoise around her swan's. Hey, lass!

ALP

(*Sniffling*) We were too happy. I knew something would happen.

SHAUN

(*Chanting*)
Three quarks for Mister Mark
Sure he hasn't got much of a bark!

EARWICKER

(*Feebly echoing him*) Mister Mark. Tristy's the spry young spark . . .

SHAUN

(*Addressing the audience*) Candidately, everybody! A mot for amot. There was this, wellyoumaycallher, a strapping modern old ancient Irish prisscess, so and so hands high, such and such paddock weight, in her madapolam smock, nothing under her hat but red hair and solid ivory . . .

SHEM

Now you know it's true in your hardup hearts!

SHAUN

And a firstclass pair of bedroom eyes, of most unhomy blue . . .

SHEM

How weak we are, one and all!

44

SHAUN

The charm of favour's fond consent! Could you blame her, we're saying, for one psocoldlogical moment?

ALP

(*Pettishly*) What would *Ewe* do? With that so tiresome old milkless a ram, with his tiresome duty peck (*she rises and takes off her widow's veils*) and his bronchial tubes, in his tiresome old twennysixandsixpenny sheopards plods drowsers and his thirtybobandninepenny tails plus toop! Ugh! (*She has removed the cloak and is now wearing a night dress. She hands the cloak and veils to Shem and lies down just below the coffin and falls asleep. In her hand she holds a small mirror. The brothers approach and stand over her.*)

SHEM

Madame Isa Veuve La Belle, so sad but lucksome in her boyblue's long black with orange blossoming weeper's veil, for she was the only girl they loved, as she is the queenly pearl you prize, because of the way the night that first we met she is bound to be, methinks, and not in vain, the darling of my heart, sleeping in her april cot, within her singachamer, with her greengageflavoured candywhistle duetted to the crazyquilt.

SHAUN

Now for la belle! Icy-la-Belle!

SHEM

Isobel, she is so pretty, truth to tell, wildwood's eyes and primarose hair, quietly, all the woods so wild, in mauves of moss and daphnedews, how all so still she lay, neath of the whitethorn, child of tree, like some losthappy leaf, like blowing flower stilled, as fain would she anon, for soon again 'twill be, win me, woo me, wed me, ah weary me! (*He lays the cloak across her tenderly.*) She is dadad's lottiest pearldaughter.

SHAUN

And brooder's cissiest auntybride.

EARWICKER

(*Echoing them*) Lottiest pearldaughter . . .

45

SHEM

To speak well her grace it would ask of Grecian language, of her goodness, that legend golden. Her shellback thimblecasket mirror only can show her dearest friendeen.

(Here A L P in the character of daughter Isobel startles them both by sitting up suddenly, holding up the mirror and gazing at her own reflection with passionate concentration. What she sees does not seem to please her. She looks very cross.)

SHAUN

(Approaching her cautiously) A tickey for tie taughts.

ALP

(In a sweet childish voice) So sorry you lost him, poor lamb! Of course I know you are a viry vikid girl to go in the dreemplace and at that time of the draym and it was a very wrong thing to do, even under the dark flush of night, dare all grandpassia!

SHAUN

The boys on the corner were talking too.

ALP

Still to forgive it, divine my lickle wiffey, and everybody knows you do look lovely in your invinsibles. *(She assumes the voice of an advertiser)* Eulogia, a perfect apposition with the coldcream, Assoluta, from Boileau's I always use in the wards after I am burned a rich egg and derive the greatest benefit, sign of the cause. *(She returns to her mirror)* My, you do! Simply adorable! Could I but pass my hands some, my hands through, thine hair! So vickyvicky veritiny!

SHEM

(Sardonically) Veriveritiny.

ALP

(Addressing her hands) O Fronces, say howdyedo, Dotty! Chic hands. The way they curve there under nue charmeen cuffs! I am more divine like that when I've two of everything up to boyproof knicks. Winning in a way, only my arms are whiter, dear. Blanchemain, idler. Fairhair, frail one. Listen, meme sweety! O be joyfold!

(*She hugs herself*) Mirror do justice, taper of ivory, heart of the cona-vent, hoops of gold! It's meemly us two, meme idoll.

SHEM

(*Reprovingly*) Sissibus, nircississies are as the doaters of inversion. Secilas through their laughing classes becoming poolermates in laker life.

ALP

(*Ignoring them both*) Of course it was downright verry wickred of him, reely meeting me disguised. How me adores eatsother simply! This is my futuous, lips and looks lovelast. (*She kisses her own re-flection.*)

SHAUN

(*Shocked*) How is this at all?

ALP

(*She rises and moves down*) Will make it up with mother Concepcion and a glorious lie between us, sweetness, so as not a novene in all the convent loretos, not my littlest one of all, for mercy's sake need ever know, what passed our lips or.

SHEM

Bansh the dread!

(*Music off: the wedding march.*)

ALP

(*Proudly*) It will all take bloss as oranged at St Audiens rosan choco-late chapelry (*she signs to Shaun to help her put on her cloak*) with my diamants blickfeast after at minne owned hos for all the catclub to go cryzy (*Shaun arranges her veil*) and Father Blesius Mindelsinn will be beminding hand. (*She is floating down the aisle in the character of Iseult. Shem waits as the bridegroom, and Shaun gives her away as the father-brother.*)

EARWICKER

(*Loudly*) Dadad's lottiest daughterpearl.

47

(*He hands a goblet to A L P*) Yes, sad one of Ziod? Sell me my soul, dear!

ALP

(*Drinking from the cup*) Now that I come to drink of it filtred, a gracecup full of bitterness (*she puts her hand to her heart*).

(*There is a roll of drums. The lights fade. The death music of "Tristan and Isolda" is heard now very softly and far away. The chapel bell begins tolling . . .*)

ALP

(*Drawing her widow's veils around her; with a great cry*) Mild und Leise! (*She dies.*)

(*Four men of the chorus enter carrying a stretcher. One of them also carries a funeral wreath in the shape of a harp. They remove their hats and stand to attention beside the body. Shem takes the wreath from them.*)

SHEM

Hear, O hear, Iseult la belle! Tristan, sad hero, hear! (*The music is louder.*) The Lambeg drum, the Lombog reed, the Lumbag fiferer, the Limibig brazenaze.

SHAUN

Hymnibusnumber twentynine, for Iseult.

SHEM, SHAUN, AND CHORUS

(*Chanting slowly and sadly*)
O, come all ye sweet nymphs of Dingle beach to cheer Brinabride
    queen from Sybil surfriding
In her curragh of shells of daughter of pearl and her silverymonnblue
    mantle round her.
Crown of the waters, brine on her brow, she'll dance them a jig and
    jilt them fairly.
Yerra, why would she bide with Sig Sloomysides or the grogram
    grey barnacle gander?
(*They raise the body and lay it on the stretcher. Shem places the wreath on the body.*)

SHEM

Here's newyearspray, the posquiflor, a windaborne and heliotrope; there miriamsweet and amaranth and maygold to crown.

CHORUS

(*Chanting*) Kyrielle elation! Crystal elation! Kyrielle elation! Elation immanse! Sing to us, sing to us, sing to us! Amam!

(*They move out as a procession to the funeral march, Shem and Shaun as chief mourners with walking sticks reversed.*)

EARWICKER

(*Despairingly*) I don't understand. I fail to say. I dearsee you too.

(*Blackout.*)

(*Much girlish laughter is heard. The lights go up and a member of the Wake rushes in carrying a white signpost on which is written, "The Fiendish Park." Another member of the chorus enters with a tree on which is one large and very red apple. The tree is placed center left and the signpost far down right. The gentleman with the signpost remains, so to speak, at his post during the ensuing scene. The tree should stand unaided. Four schoolgirls run in laughing and chattering. They wear convent-school uniforms and carry small folding chairs which they set up under or around the tree and then stand to attention behind them.*
Shaun bounces in, a dashing figure full of fire and energy. He stands center, twirling his cane. The girls greet him with screams of admiration.)

MAN WITH SIGNPOST

Introducing Jaunty Jaun. Amply altered for the brighter, though still the graven image of his squarer self . . . Now, there were as many as twentynine hedge daughters out of Benent Saint Berched's national nightschool learning their antemeridian lesson of life, under its tree, against its warning, O so jaonickally, all barely in their typtap teens.

SHAUN

(*Enveloped by girls*) And where's Agatha's lamb? (*Tickling and pinching them all through his kind inquiries*) and how are Bernadetta's

49

columbillas? and Juliennaw's tubberbunnies? and Eulalina's tugger-
funnies?

MAN WITH SIGNPOST

Jaun, by the way, was by the way of becoming (I think, I hope he
was) the most purely human being that ever was called man, loving
all up and down the whole creation from Sampson's tyke to Jones's
sprat.

SHAUN

(*Becoming very dignified and taking on the manner of a Savonarola*)
I rise, O fair assemblage! Andcommincio. (*Motions the girls to be
seated; whispering excitedly, they obey him*) Now then, after this introit
of exordium, my galaxy girls, comeallyedimseldamsels, siddle down
and lissle all!

GIRLS

(*Sighing*) Oh yes, Professor.

SHAUN

Follow me close! Keep me in view! Understeady me saries! Now.
During our brief apsence from this furtive feugtig season adhere to
as many as probable of the ten commandments touching purgations
and indulgences and in the long run they will prove for your better
guidance along your path of right of way. Where the lisieuse are
we and what's the first sing to be sung? Ah! Never play lady's game
for the Lord's stake. Never lose your heart away till you win his
diamond back. First thou shalt not smile. Twice thou shalt not love.
Lust, thou shalt not commix idolatry. Hip confiners help compunc-
tion. Never slip the silver key through your gate of golden age.
Collide with man, collude with money. And look before you leak,
dears.

GIRLS

Oh yes, Professor.

SHAUN

Sisters, I'd burn the books that grieve you and light an allassundrian
bompyre that would suffragate Tome Plyfire or Zolfanerole. Pe-
rousse instate your *Weekly Standerd*, our verile organ that is ethelred

by all pressdom. Give back those stolen kisses; restaure those all-cotten glooves. Stick wicks in your earshells when you hear the prompter's voice. I cannot belabour the point too ardently (and after the lessions of experience I speak from inspiration) that fetid spirits is the thief of prurities, so none of your twenty rod cherry-whisks, me daughter!

GIRLS

No, Professor. No. No. No.

SHAUN

(*Fiercely*) Once and for all, I'll have no college swankies trespassing on your danger zone in the dancer years. If ever I catch you nosing around with that rogues' gallery of dosed, doctored and belegalized bitchfanciers, I'll give it to you, hot, high and heavy before you can say sedro!

GIRLS

No, Professor; yes, Professor; no, Professor. Yes. Yes. Yes.

SHAUN

Sisters, there is some thing more. A word apparting and shall the heart's tone be silent. Mark this ye hefty hoydens . . .

GIRLS

Oh, Professor.

SHAUN

The pleasures of love lasts but a fleeting but the pledges of life out-lusts a lieftime. (*The girls sigh.*) The Vico road goes round and round to meet where terms begin. Still onappealed to by the cycles and unappalled by the recoursers we feel all serene, never you fret, as regards our dutyful cask. (*He jigs a few steps, twirls the cane, lifts his hat, replaces it, and continues*) I'll lay you a guinea for a hayseed now. Tell mother that. And tell her tell her old one. T'will amuse her. (*He laughs heartily.*)

GIRLS

(*Greatly encouraged*) Oh yes, Professor. Yes. Yes. Yes.

51

(A L P runs in and impulsively flings her arms around him. She is wearing the uniform of Benent St. Berched's Nightschool.)

ALP

Listen, Jaunick, accept this witwee's mite, though a jennyteeny witween piece torn in one place from my hands in second place of a linenhall valentino with my fondest and much left to tutor.

SHAUN

(Enraged) Izzy! I overstand you, you understand. Cutting chapel, were you? and had dates with slickers in particular hotels, had we? Lonely went to play your mother, isod? You was wiffriends? Hay, dot's a doll yarn! Mark mean then! *(He laughs. The girls laugh, all except poor Izzy who slinks back to her seat in tears.)* All I can tell you is this, my sorellies. It's prayers in layers all the thumping time, begor, the young gloria's gang voices the old doxologers, in the suburrs of the heavenly gardens, once we shall have passed, after surceases, all serene through neck and necklike Derby and June to our snug eternal retribution's reward (the scorchhouse). Allmen!

GIRLS

Allmen. Ahmen. *(Passionately)* Men!

SHAUN

(Becoming very personal) Well, here's looking at ye! If I never leave you biddies till my stave is a bar I'd be tempted rigidly to become a passionate father.

GIRLS

Oh, Professor.

SHAUN

(Pinching the weeping one) Me hunger's weighed. Hungkung! Me anger's suaged! Hangkang!

ALP

(Gratefully) Oh thank you, Professor.

SHAUN

Ye can stop as ye are, little lay mothers, and wait in wish and wish in vain till the grame reaper draws nigh, with the sickle of the sickles, as a blessing in disguise. Allmen.

(*Shem enters, stands beside Shaun.*)

SHEM

Eh jourd'weh! Oh jourd'woe! A dream of favours, a favourable dream. They know how they believe that they believe that they know. Wherefore they wail.

(*The girls stand up, fold chairs, and wait reverently with heads bowed.*)

SHEM

(*Removes hat, stands with head bowed*) Oasis, cedarous esaltarshoming Leafboughnoon!

SHAUN AND THE GIRLS

Oisis, coolpressus onmountof Sighing!

SHEM

Oasis, palmost esaltarshoming Gladdays!

SHAUN AND THE GIRLS

Oisis, phantastichal roseway anjerichol!

SHEM

Oasis, newleavos spaciosing encampness!

SHAUN AND THE GIRLS

Oisis, plantainous dewstuckacqmirage playtennis!

SHEM

Pipetto, Pipetta has misery unnoticed!

SHAUN

(*Replacing hat and becoming extremely jovial*) Well, my positively last at any stage! I hate to look at alarms but however they put on my watchcraft must now close. The earth's atrot! The sun's a scream!

53

The air's a jig. The water's great! (*He jigs a few steps, then stops, groaning with foot trouble*) I'm going. I know I am. (*Raises stick as if it were a sword*) Lead on, Macadam, and danked be he who first sights Halt Linduff! Come, my good frogmarchers. (*He marshals the girls in front of him.*)

GIRLS

(*Fading*) Solo, solone, solong . . . (*The signpost and the tree exit. Shaun picks the apple as it passes.*)

SHAUN

(*Limping*) Break ranks! Fik yew! I'm through. Won. You watch my smoke.

(*The girls stand aside to let him pass. He goes eating the apple. The girls march out after him.*)

EARWICKER

(*Very restless*) What was thaas? Fog was whaas? Too mult sleepth. Let sleepth.

(*The light begins fading.*)

SHEM

Wethen, now, may the good people speed you, rural Haun, export stout fellow that you are, the crooner born with sweet wail of evoker, healing music, ay, and heart in hand of Shamrogueshire! Brave footsore Haun! Work your progress! Hold to! Now! Win out, ye divil ye! The silent cock shall crow at last. The west shall shake the east awake. Walk while ye have the night for morn, lightbreakfastbringer, morroweth whereon every past shall full fost sleep.

(*Blackout. We now hear the chimes of a college chapel bell. The male members of the Wake start moving in and seating themselves below the coffin. Their voices come out of the darkness.*)

CHORUS

(*As they enter*)
Xanthos! Xanthos! Xanthos!
Today. Preausteric man and his pursuit of panhysteric woman.

Early notions of acquired rights and the influence of collective tradi-
tion upon the individual.
Move up, Mackinerny! Make room for Muckinurney!
Bags! Balls!

*(The lights rise now on the men sitting as in a seminary classroom
listening or appearing to listen to a young professor of canon law, Shem,
in fact, who now wears clerical black over his tennis flannels. Shaun
has also joined the class.)*

SHEM

(Consulting his notes) The procurator Interrogarius Mealterum pre-
sends us this proposer . . . *(coughs gently)*.

SHAUN

(Rising and addressing the world) Bet you fippence, anythesious,
there's no purgatory, are yous game?

(Cheers from chorus.)

SHEM

Honuphrius is a concupiscent exservicemajor who makes dis-
honest propositions to all. *(Cheers from chorus and a roll of drums
off. Shem continues unperturbed, though Earwicker sits up, looks wildly
round, and lies down.)* He is considered to have committed, invoking
droit d'oreiller, simple infidelities with Felicia, a virgin. Anita the
wife of Honophrius, has been told by her tirewoman, Fortissa, that
Honophrius has blasphemously confessed under voluntary chas-
tisement that he has instructed his slave, Mauritius, to urge Magravius, a commercial, emulous of Honuphrius, to solicit the chastity
of Anita. *(He pauses for breath.)*

SHAUN

I've lost the place, where was I?

SHEM

Anita is informed by some illegitimate children of Fortissa with
Mauritius (the supposition is Ware's) that Gillia, the schismatical
wife of Magravius has been corrupted by Jeremias. Gillia, (a cooler

55

blend, D'Alton insists) *ex equo* with Marinuzza, Indra and Iodina, has been tenderly debauched (in Halliday's view), by Honuphrius!

(*Low whistles from the students, and Shem in a state of intolerable confusion shuffles through his notes. Earwicker sits up.*)

EARWICKER

(*Gazing at Shem*) I don't understand. Holy policeman, O I see . . . (*falls back*).

SHEM

(*Recovering himself*) Anita has formerly committed double sacrilege with Michael, *vulgo* Cerularius, a perpetual curate, who wishes to seduce Eugenius. Magravius threatens to have Anita molested by Sulla, an orthodox savage (and leader of a band of twelve mercenaries, the Sullivani) (*Loud cries of "Up the Sullivans." Shem delicately raises his hand for silence.*) who desires to procure Felicia for Gregorius, Leo, Vitellius and Macdugalius, four excavators, if she will not yield to him . . .

MEMBER OF CHORUS

(*Standing up*) Tickets for the Tailwaggers Terrierpuppy Raffle?

SHEM

(*Once more motioning for silence*) Anita is disturbed but Michael comminates that he will reserve her case tomorrow for the ordinary Guglielmus even if she should practise a pious fraud during affrication which, from experience, she knows (according to Wadding), to be leading to nullity. Fortissa, however, is encouraged by Gregorius, Leo, Viteilius, and —

CHORUS

MacDougal!

(*Lights fade.*)

SHEM

Reunitedly, to warn Anita by describing the strong chastisements of Honuphrius and the depravities (*turpissimas!*) of Canicula, the deceased wife of Mauritius, with Sulla, the simoniac, who is abnegand and repents. Has he hegemony and shall she submit?

56

(*Diminuendo as they file out*) Noah. Plato. Horace. Tiresias. Marius. Diogenes. Procne. Philomela. Sappho. Moses. (*We hear the chimes again as they disappear followed by Shaun.*)

EARWICKER

(*Sitting up*) Something happened that time I was asleep, torn letters or was there snow? (*He lies down again and snores.*)

(*Blackout and a drum roll.*)

RADIO ANNOUNCER

Order. Order. Translate a lax, you breed a bradaun. In the goods of Cape and Chattertone, deceased . . .

VOICE

(*Echoing him*) In the goods of Cape and Chattertone, deceased.

VOICES

(*Crescendo as they file in*) Doyle, Doyle, Doyle, Doyle, Doyle, Doyle . . .

(*The lights come up on a professor of civil law, Shem again, a more earthy type than the last lecturer, presenting a case to a group of law students. Shem — the Professor — and his audience all wear barristers' wigs and gowns. Again there are no ladies present — at present!*)

SHEM

(*In a thundering brogue*) This, lay readers and gentilemen, is perhaps the commonest of all cases arising out of umbrella history in connection with the wood industries in our courts of litigation.

SHAUN

(*Making notes*) Glory be to Saint Patrick! What is to be found in this dustheap? The value of circumstantial evidence?

SHEM

(*Pacing*) D'Oyley Owens holds (though Finn Magnusson of himself holds also) that so long as there is a joint deposit account in the two names a mutual obligation is posted. Owens cites Brerfuchs and Warren, a foreign firm, since disseized, registered as Tangos,

Limited (*cymbals followed by the drum beating a tango rhythm*), for the sale of certain proprietary articles. The action which was at the instance of the trustee of the heathen church emergency fund, suing by its trustee, a resigned civil servant . . .

(*He remains frozen, as does the class. Two girls have rushed in, and they begin to remove their blouses as they talk.*)

FIRST GIRL

(*Pointing rudely at Shem*) He's as mad as the brambles he is! He has kissed me more than once, I am sorry to say and if I did commit gladrolleries, may the loone forgive it!

SECOND GIRL

I believe you. Taiptope reelly, O reelly!

(*They disappear and the class comes to life.*)

SHEM

For the payment of tithes due was heard by Judge Doyle and also by a common jury.

SHAUN

The haves and the havenots: a distinction!

SHEM

The bank particularised, the national misery (now almost entirely in the hands of the four chief bondholders for value in Tangos) . . .

(*We're off again. The drum begins beating the tango rhythm.*)

Declined to pay the draft, though there were ample reserves to meet the liability . . .

(*Two more girls run in, unbuttoning their blouses, as they talk.*)

FIRST GIRL

O wait till I tell you!

SECOND GIRL

We are not going yet (*pointing at the class*). Excuse theyre christian-brothers irish.

FIRST GIRL

Here's what he done that fellow; as snooks as I am saying so . . .

(*They vanish and the class comes to life.*)

SHEM

Though there were ample reserves to meet the liability, whereupon the trusty Coppercheap negociated it for and on behalf of the fund of the thing to a client of his, a notary, from whom, on consideration, he received in exchange legal relief as between trusthee and bethrust, with thanks. Now the jury — a sour dozen —

(*The drum again begins the tango rhythm.*)

And only the junior partner Barren could be found, who entered an appearance and turned up, upon notice . . .

(*Two girls rush in and remove their skirts. Since they have already removed their blouses, the class shows increasing excitement and even Shem feels the strain.*)

FIRST GIRL

(*Lyrically*) Poor Isa sits a glooming so gleaming in the gloaming! Her beauman's gone of a cool. Be good enough to symperise. If he's at anywhere she's therefor to join him. If it's to nowhere she's going to too. Buf if he'll go to be a son to France's she'll stay daughter of Clare.

SECOND GIRL

(*Vaguely*) Bring tansy, throw myrtle, strew rue, rue, rue . . . (*They go.*)

SHEM

Upon notice of motion and after service of the motion by interlocutory injunction, among the male jurors to be an absolete turfwoman, originally from the proletarian class, with still a good title to her sexname of Ann Doyle, 2 Coppinger's Cottages.

SHAUN

We're now entering the Doyle country.

(*The class takes the address eagerly.*)

59

Ann Doyle having regretfully left the juryboxers, protested cheerfully on the stand in a long jurymiad *in re* corset checks, and of how she had been made at sight for services rendered the payeedrawee of unwashable blank assignations, sometimes pinkwilliams.

(*Much laughter from class.*)

SHAUN

Finny. Vary vary finny!

SHEM

The witness, at her own request, asked if she might and wrought something between the sheets (*whistles from the class*) of music paper which she had accompanied herself with for the occasion and this having been handed up for the bench to look at *in camera*, Coppinger's doll, as she was called, was handed down to the jury of the Liffey that, as a matter of tact, the woman they gave as free was born into contractual incapacity (the Calif of Man *v* the Eaudelusk Company) when, how and where mamy's mancipium act did not apply and therefore held supremely that, as no property in law can exist in a corpse . . .

(*All freeze into position.*)

EARWICKER

(*Rising*) Let op. Slew musies. Thunner in the eire. (*Goes back to sleep.*)

SHEM

(*Demented*) (Hal Kilbride *v* Una Bellina) Pepigi's pact was pure piffle (*loud laughter*) and Wharrem would whistle for the rhino.

(*The girls enter in neat little sun suits to the usual tango rhythm and beating of drums. They stand center. The lights begin fading.*)

SHEM

Will you, won't you, pango with Pepigi? (*He begins dancing to the rhythm*) Not for Nancy, how dare you do!

Whew whewwhew whew.

(*The class is up now and swaying in time to the music. There is a clash of cymbals; all the dancers freeze into immobility and one of the girls rushes on. She is wearing a large placard with NIGHTLETTER written on it. She takes a letter out of her bosom and hands it to Shem, who reads it aloud very slowly and distinctly and facing the audience.*)

SHEM

"With our best youlldied greedings to Pep and Memmy and the old folkers below and beyant, wishing them all very merry Incarnations in this land of the livvey, and plenty or preposperousness through their coming new yonks. From jake, jack and little souscouci (the babes that mean too). Sender. Boston. Mass."

(*Earwicker wakes slowly, rises from his bed. The chorus cheers at the conclusion of the reading.*)

SHAUN

(*Shouting*) Sponsor program and close down.

(*Blackout*)

CURTAIN

SCENE SIX

Two members of the Wake step out in front of the curtains. They stand as in Scene One, and they are the same two characters.

FIRST DUBLINER

(*Intoning as in prayer*) Prospector projector and boomooster giant builder of all causeways woesoever . . .

SECOND DUBLINER

(*Also intoning*) Big Maester Finnykin with Phenicia Parkes, lame of his ear and gape of her leg, most correctingly, we beseach of you, down their laddercase of nightwatch service and bring them at suntime flush with the nethermost gangrung of their stepchildren, guide them through the labyrinth of their samilikes and the alteregoases of their pseudoselves, hedge them bothways from all roamers whose names are ligious, from loss of bearings deliver them . . .

FIRST DUBLINER

That he may dishcover her, that she may uncouple him, that one may come and crumple them, that they may soon recoup themselves: now and then, time on time again . . .

SECOND DUBLINER

At shipside, by convent garden: monk and sempstress, in sackcloth silkily: curious dreamers, curious dramas, curious deman, plagiast dayman, playajest dearest, plaguiest dourest . . .

(*The hunting horn blows from far away. They both stop and listen.*)

FIRST DUBLINER

(*In great excitement*) He's rounding up on his family.

(*As usual avid for news*) And who is the bodikin by him, sir?

Why, that's old missness wipethemdry.

Which route are they going? Why?

Angell sitter or Amen Corner, Norwood's Southwalk or Euston Waste? The solvent man in his upper gambeson withnot a breth against him and the wee wiping womanahoussy. They're coming terug their diamond wedding tour, down the scales, the way they went up . . .

Oil's wells in our lands. Let earwigger's wivable teach you the dance!

(*The curtains part revealing the chorus seated around the stage in various attitudes of sleep. The coffin is down center again, but it is now a cradle and beside it sits a shawled woman, A L P, moving it gently and crooning a lullaby. Earwicker, now awake, stands beside A L P and Shaun and Shem are seated on either side of the coffin-cradle.*)

Now their laws assist them and ease their fall. (*Both Dubliners softly join the sleeping Wake.*)

(*Tenderly*) For they met and mated and bedded and buckled and got and gave and reared and raised and brought Thawland within Har danger, and turned them, tarrying to the sea and planted and plundered and pawned our souls and pillaged the pounds of the extramurals and fought and feigned with strained relations and turned out coats and removed their origins and never learned the first day's lesson and tried to mingle and managed to save and feathered foes' nests and fouled their own . . .

Till their hour with their scene be struck for ever and the book of the dates he close, he clasp and she and she seegn her tour d'adieu (*horn faintly in distance*), Pervinca calling . . . O Sheem!

SHEM

O Shaam! And gentle Isad Ysut gag, flispering in the nightleaves flattery, dinsiduously, to Finnegan, to sin again and to make grim grandma grunt and grin again while the first grey streaks steal silvering by for to mock their quarrels in dollymount tumbling . . .

CHORUS

They near the base of the chill stair.

(*Lullaby sung by the women*)
October winds lament around the Castle of Dromore
Yet peace is in its lofty halls, my dearest treasure store?
Though autumn leaves may droop and die
A bud of spring are you —

Sing hushaby, lul lul lo lo lan,
Sing hushaby, lul lul loo.

Bring no ill will to hinder us, my helpless babe and me
Dread spirit of Blackwater banks, Clan Eoghan's wild banshee;
And Holy Mary, pitying us, in heaven for grace doth sue —

Sing hushaby, lul lul lo lo lan,
Sing hushaby, lul lul loo.

Take time to thrive, my rose of hope,
In the garden of Dromore;
Take heed young eagle — till your wings
Are feathered fit to soar;
A little rest and then the world
Is full of work to do.

Sing hushaby, lul lul lo lo lan,
Sing hushaby lul lul loo.

WOMEN'S VOICES

(*Whispering*) He sighed in sleep. Let us go back, lest he forewaken. Hide ourselves . . .

ALP

While hovering dreamwings, folding around, will hide from fears
my wee mee mannikin, keep my big wig long strong manomen,
guard my bairn, *mon beau.*

SHEM

(*Beside A L P*) Lead, kindly fowl! They always did: ask the ages.
What bird has done yesterday man may do next year, be it fly, be
it moult, be it hatch, be it agreement in the nest. For her socio-
scientific sense is sound as a bell, sir, her volucrine automutativeness
right on normalcy: she knows, she just feels she was kind of born to
lay and love eggs (trust her to propagate the species and hoosh her
fluffballs safe through din and danger!); lastly but mostly, in her
genesic field it is all game and no gammon; she is ladylike in everything she does and plays the gentleman's part every time. Let us
auspice it! Yes, before all this has time to end the golden age must
return with its vengeance. Man will become dirigible, Ague will be
rejuvenated, woman with her ridiculous white burden will reach
by one step sublime incubation, the manewanting human lioness
with her dishorned discipular manram will lie down together publicly
flank upon fleece.

(*The horn blows again; this time much nearer.*)

ALP

(*To the sleeping child*) He is quieter now.

EARWICKER

Legalentitled. Accesstopartnuzz. Notwildebeestsch. Byrightofoaptz.
Twainbeonerflsh. Haveandholdpp.

ALP

You were dreamend, dear. The pawdrag? The fawthrig? Shoe! Hear
are no phanthares in the room at all, avikkeen. No bad bold faathern,
dear one.

WOMEN'S VOICES

— *Li ne dormis?*
— *S! Malbone dormas.*
— *Kia li krias nikte?*
— *Parolas infanetes. S!*

65

(*Looking down at the child*) Sonly all in your imagination, dim. Poor little brittle magic nation, dim of mind! Shoe to me now, dear! Shoom of me! While elvery stream winds seling on for to keep this barrel of bounty rolling and the nightmail afarfrom morning nears . . .

WOMEN'S VOICES

Hear no more those voices, always I'm hearing them.

MEN'S VOICES

Remember. What has gone? How it ends?

SHEM

Begin to forget it. It will remember itself from every sides, with all gestures, in each our word. Today's truth, tomorrow's trend.

MEN'S VOICES

Forget, remember!

(*The light changes slowly to day.*)

SHEM

Have we cherished expectations? Are we for liberty of perusiveness?

SHAUN

Whyafter what forewhere?

MEN'S VOICES

Forget! . . . Cocorico! (*The cock crows.*)

EARWICKER

(*Loudly*) Hues of rich unfolding morn. Wake up; rise and prove. Provide for sacrifice. (*The horn blows.*) Come all ye goatfathers and groanmothers, come all ye markmakers and piledrivers, come all ye laboursaving devisers and chargeleyden dividends, firefinders, water-workers, deeply condeal with him! All that is still life with death inyeborn, all verbumsaps yet bound to be, to do and to suffer, every creature, everywhere, if you please, kindly feel for her! While the dapplegray dawn drags nearing nigh for to wake all droners that drowse in Dublin.

Sandhyas! Sandhyas! Sandhyas! Calling all downs. Calling all downs to dayne. Array! Surrection!

CHORUS

(*Waking up*) Array! Array!

EARWICKER

(*In great joy*) Eireweeker to the wohld bludyn world. O rally, O rally, O rally! The smog is lofting. (*He goes.*)

(*The hunting horn is heard. The chorus led by Shem and Shaun sings the chorus of "John Peel." Shaun takes Earwicker's place center below A L P.*)

SHEM

(*Introducing Shaun to the world*) Here gives your answer, pigs and scuts! Hence we've lived in two worlds. He is another he what stays under the himp of holth. The herewaker of our hamefame is his real name-same who will get himself up and erect (*he looks down at the coffin-cradle*), confident and heroic when but, young as of old, for my daily comfreshenall, a wee one woos.

(*Blackout and music, during which the chorus parades around the coffin masking the return of the corpse. They sing the last verse of "Persse O'Reilly," and they then take up their positions as in Scene One. A L P stands above them now and one spot shines upon her. She has become an old tired woman. The chorus turns to her.*)

CHORUS

(*Lovingly*) Anna Livia Plurabelle, that our turfbrown mummy is acoming . . . Beside the hithering waters of, the hitherandthithering waters of . . . (*they sink down and only A L P is lighted*).

ALP

Soft morning, city! Lsp! I am leafy speafing. Lpf! Folty and folty all the nights have fallen on to long my hair. Not a sound, falling. Lispn! No wind no word. Only a leaf, just a leaf and then leaves. The woods are fond always. Away! Rise up, man of the hooths, you have slept so long! Rise up now and aruse! Norvena's over. I am leafy, your goolden, so you called me, may be life, yea your goolden, silve me solve, exsogerraider! You did so drool. I was so sharm. But there's a great poet in you too. And people thinks you missed the scaffold. Of fell design. I'll close me eyes. So not to see. Or see only a youth in his florizel, a boy in innocence, peeling a twig, a child beside a weenywhite steed. The child we all love to place our hope in for ever. All men has done something. Be the time they've come to the weight of old fletch. We'll lave it. So. But you're changing accolsha, you're changing from me, I can feel. (*She pulls her cloak around her and becomes older, more remote.*) Or is it me is? I'm getting mixed. Brightening up and tightening down. I pity your oldself I was used to. Now a younger's there. Try not to part! Be happy, dear ones! May I be wrong! For she'll be sweet for you as I was sweet when I came down out of me mother. My great blue bedroom, the air so quiet, scarce a cloud. In peace and silence. I could have stayed up there for always only. It's something fails us. First we feel. Then we fall. And let her rain now if she likes. Gently or strongly as she likes. Anyway let her rain for my time is come. I done me best when I was let. Thinking always if I go all goes. A hundred cares, a tithe of troubles and is there one who understands me? One in a thousand of years of the nights? All me life I have been lived among them but now they are becoming lothed to me. And I am lothing their little warm tricks. And lothing their mean cosy turns. And all the greedy gushes out through their small souls. And all the lazy leaks down over their brash bodies. How small it's all! And me letting on to meself always. And lilting on all the time. I thought you were all glittering with the noblest of carriage. You're only a bumpkin. I thought you the great in all things, in guilt and in glory. You're but a puny. Home! My people were not their sort out beyond there so far as I can. For all the bold and bad and bleary they are blamed, the seahags. No! Nor for all our wild dances in all their wild din. I can seen meself among them, allaniuvia pulchrabelled. How she was handsome, the wild Amazia, when she would seize to my other breast! And what is she weird, haughty Niluna, that she will snatch from my ownest hair! For 'tis they are the stormies. Ho hang! Hang ho! And the clash of our cries till we spring to be free. Auravoles, they says, never heed of your name! But I'm loothing them that's here and all I lothe. Loonely in me loneness. For all their faults. I am passing out. O bitter ending! I'll slip away before they're up. (*Music very soft*) They'll never see. Nor know. Nor miss me. And

68

it's old and old it's sad and old it's sad and weary I go back to you, my cold father, my cold mad father, my cold mad feary father, till the near sight of the mere size of him, the moyles and moyles of it, moananoaning, makes me seasilt saltsick and I rush, my only, into your arms. I see them rising! Save me from those therrble prongs! Two more. Onetwo moremens more. So. Avelaval. My leaves have drifted from me. All. But one clings still. I'll bear it on me. To re-mind me of. Lff! So soft this morning, ours. Yes. Carry me along, taddy, like you done through the toy fair! If I seen him bearing down on me now under whitespread wings like he'd come from Arkangels, I sink I'd die down over his feet, humbly dumbly, only to washup. Yes, tid. There's where. First. We pass through grass behush the bush to. (*Music and sound of gulls*) Whish! A gull. Gulls. Far calls. Coming, far! End here. Us then. Finn, again! Take. Bussoftlhee, mememormee! Till thousendsthee. Lps. The keys to. Given! A way a lone a last a loved a long the

(*Darkness.*)

(*The lights come up and the Wake is revealed exactly as it was in the opening scene.*)

CHORUS

(*Very softly*) riverrun, past Eve and Adam's, from swerve of shore to bend of bay, brings us by a commodius vicus of recirculation back to Howth Castle and Environs.

(*The horn blows far away.*)

CURTAIN

PRODUCTION NOTE

Versatile actors, clever and imaginative lighting, ingenious sound effects are essential to this production of *Finnegans Wake.* The words are the things indeed and the words should be sacred. Perfect audibility is required and the most loving training of the choral passages. Joyce wrote to be heard. Any production of *Finnegan* should be paced so that the audience has time to hear. If not, the subtle imagery, adroit punning, and the essential meaning will be lost in a verbal shuffle. True, we have used ballet, but here again the words dominate the dancers.

The dream dramas at the conclusion of the Jaunty Jaun sequence should move very fast and the interpolations from the chorus must merge into or be heard above the Professor's speeches. From here on the scene is a *danse macabre* with words until the stage freezes into position for the reading of the letter. Then, the moment we see Earwicker awake and rising from his bed, comes the blackout and Shaun brings the curtain down on the dream.

The Anna Livia speech at the end must *not* be acted; it must flow simply and inevitably as the river "old tird and weary" flows out to sea.

The ballads used in the various scenes can be found in many collections and are all easily procured from records, or in college and public libraries. The "Ballad of Persse O'Reilly" is in *Finnegans Wake* (with the music), as is the hymn for Iseult. The songs are carefully chosen because they are, except the lullaby, all woven into the book in some form or other and are part of the Dublin life Joyce knew so well and remembered with such passionate accuracy. The lullaby is a late eighteenth-century county Cork ballad and is a great favorite in Ireland still. I do not think its use would have offended Joyce.

71

It is important that any director of *Finnegan* should avoid phoney brogues. Joyce has given the actor everything he needs; by clever phonetical spelling and rhythmical arrangements of sentences he has produced the lilting drawl of the Dubliner. Stage Irishisms would inevitably vulgarize the production. *Finnegan* has little to do with leprechauns, wee folk, or indeed, any shamroguery. There were no roses round the door of "the Haunted Inkbottle, no number, Brimstone Walk, Asia in Ireland."

M. M.

ACKNOWLEDGMENTS

I wish to express my thanks to Professor Robert Chapman, who first inspired me with the idea of this adaptation during our work with the Actor's Lab at Harvard; to Professors Harry T. Levin and John V. Kelleher for their wise counsel and generous help; to my friend Denis Johnston for much encouragement, when I needed it; to my friends and co-workers in the Poets' Theatre, especially Edward Thommen, who *directed* Finnegan with infectious and endearing enthusiasm so that a perfect coöperation was formed between adapter and director; to Roger Graef, who composed a music score for the Actor's Lab production; to Stanley Spector, who composed the splendid percussion music used in the New York production; and to Nora White Shattuck, tireless worker and a choreographer with a sense of humor. And above all to those on the home-front who had to endure the birthpangs of this adaptation.

Cambridge, Massachusetts   M. M.
1957

Cast of first production by the Poets' Theatre in Cambridge
on April 25, 1955

Finnegan	Joseph Mitchell
Earwicker	Ken Donahue
Shem	Tom Clancy
Shaun	Ed Chamberlain
A L P (*Anna Livia Plurabelle*)	Sarah Braveman

Members of the Wake, who played various roles,
Jack Rogers, Edward Thommen, Henry Fitz-
patrick, Jay Shuchter, Kitty Beer, Patricia Guest,
Joanna Hutchins, Grace Tuttle, Lisa Rosenfarb

Directed by Edward Thommen
Choreography by Nora White Shattuck
*Original music for voice, drum, flute, and recorder
composed and played by* Roger Graef

75